As a MAN
THINKETH

Revised and Updated for the Twenty-first Century

Includes

From POVERTY
to POWER

JEREMY P. TARCHER/PENGUIN
a member of Penguin Group (USA) Inc.
New York

As a MAN THINKETH

&

From POVERTY to POWER

JAMES ALLEN

Revised and Updated for the Twenty-first Century
by Arthur R. Pell, Ph.D.

JEREMY P. TARCHER/PENGUIN
Published by the Penguin Group
Penguin Group (USA) Inc., 375 Hudson Street, New York, New York 10014, USA • Penguin Group
(Canada), 90 Eglinton Avenue East, Suite 700, Toronto, Ontario M4P 2Y3, Canada (a division of Pearson
Canada Inc.) • Penguin Books Ltd, 80 Strand, London WC2R 0RL, England • Penguin Ireland,
25 St Stephen's Green, Dublin 2, Ireland (a division of Penguin Books Ltd) • Penguin Group
(Australia), 250 Camberwell Road, Camberwell, Victoria 3124, Australia (a division of Pearson Australia
Group Pty Ltd) • Penguin Books India Pvt Ltd, 11 Community Centre, Panchsheel Park,
New Delhi–110 017, India • Penguin Group (NZ), 67 Apollo Drive, Rosedale, North Shore 0632,
New Zealand (a division of Pearson New Zealand Ltd) • Penguin Books (South Africa) (Pty) Ltd,
24 Sturdee Avenue, Rosebank, Johannesburg 2196, South Africa

Penguin Books Ltd, Registered Offices: 80 Strand, London WC2R 0RL, England

From Poverty to Power originally published in 1901
As a Man Thinketh originally published in 1903
First Jeremy P. Tarcher/Penguin editions published 2008

As a Man Thinketh revision © 2008 by JMW Group, Inc.
From Poverty to Power revision © 2008 by JMW Group, Inc.

Most Tarcher/Penguin books are available at special quantity discounts for bulk purchase for sales
promotions, premiums, fund-raising, and educational needs. Special books or book excerpts also can be
created to fit specific needs. For details, write Penguin Group (USA) Inc. Special Markets, 375 Hudson
Street, New York, NY 10014.

ISBN 978-1-58542-638-6

Printed in the United States of America
9   10   8

While the author has made every effort to provide accurate telephone numbers and Internet addresses at
the time of publication, neither the publisher nor the author assumes any responsibility for errors, or for
changes that occur after publication. Further, the publisher does not have any control over and does not
assume any responsibility for author or third-party websites or their content.

Neither the publisher nor the author is engaged in rendering professional advice or services to the
individual reader. The ideas, procedures, and suggestions contained in this book are not intended as a
substitute for consulting with a physician. All matters regarding your health require medical supervision.
Neither the author nor the publisher shall be liable or responsible for any loss or damage allegedly arising
from any information or suggestion in this book.

INTRODUCTION

to the Tarcher/Penguin Edition

by Arthur R. Pell, Ph.D.

Many books have been written that inspire readers to take action that will truly improve their lives. In the twentieth century, dozens of these writings have become best sellers and catapulted their authors to international fame. Books by Dale Carnegie, Norman Vincent Peale, Joshua Loth Liebman, Tony Robbins, and others have improved the lives of millions of men and women.

Probably one of the first of these motivational writers, the one who, indeed, opened the door to what is now called the human potential movement, the man whose writings were the wellspring from which this philosophy was generated, was James Allen.

James Allen was born in Leicester, England, in 1864.

Orphaned as a young child, he had to work and educate himself, and as an adult he earned his living in clerical and administrative work. He was an avid reader and studied the works of the great Russian writer Leo Tolstoy, as well as the new studies in science by Charles Darwin, and others of his generation. Allen also immersed himself in reading about religions—not only his own Christian faith but also the Eastern religions Buddhism, Hinduism, and Confucianism.

In 1902 he gave up his clerical job to devote himself fully to his writing. He proved brilliantly prolific, completing nineteen inspirational works before his unfortunately early death at age forty-eight in 1912.

His concepts were developed from his strong belief in the teachings of the Bible on the one hand, and in the ideas of the Asian religions on the other. For example, his most famous work, *As a Man Thinketh,* took its title from the biblical book of Proverbs, but Buddha commented similarly, "All that we are is the result of what we have thought."

The theme of all of Allen's works is that each one of us has the power to form our own character and to create our own happiness. The conditions of our lives are closely related to our inner state. Allen encourages his readers to think positive thoughts, which will inevitably lead them to take positive actions.

Two of Allen's nineteen books are included in this volume. *As a Man Thinketh* is by far his best-known work. In an easy-to-read inspirational style, this short work provides a formula for achieving a better life and practical steps from which to begin.

From Poverty to Power is a deeper reflection on the theme of self-development. Its philosophy is that none of us is doomed to live the life we now have and that we possess within ourselves the power to alter our lives for the better.

Read each book with a generous spirit. You may not agree with everything—and indeed some of Allen's ideals have not been realized in modern times. But many of his concepts are as meaningful today as they were when he wrote them one hundred years ago. But don't just read these volumes and then tuck them away on your bookshelf. These are books that should be reread periodically, books that will continually inspire you. And when you apply what you read in them, your life can be greatly enriched.

As a MAN THINKETH

"Mind is the Master power that molds and makes,
And Man is Mind, and evermore he takes
The tool of Thought, and, shaping what he wills,
Brings forth a thousand joys, a thousand ills.
He thinks in secret, and it comes to pass:
Environment is but his looking glass."

CONTENTS

THOUGHT AND CHARACTER

The Book of Proverbs (23:7) proclaims, "As a man thinketh in his heart, so is he." This adage reaches out to every condition and circumstance of human endeavor. Each of us is literally *what we think,* our character being the complete sum of all our thoughts.

As the plant springs from and could not be without the seed, so every one of our acts springs from the hidden seeds of thought and could not have appeared without them. This applies equally to those acts called spontaneous and unpremeditated as to those that are deliberately executed.

Action is the blossom of thought, and joy and suffering are its fruits; thus do we garner in the sweet and bitter harvest of our own plantings. We are what we think we are. If our mind has evil thoughts, we will suffer pain; if our thoughts are pure, joy will follow.

Human growth is a natural phenomenon and not a creation by artifice. Cause and effect is as absolute and undeviating in the hidden realm of thought as in the world of visible and material things. A noble and God-like character is not a thing of favor or chance but is the natural result of continuous effort and right thinking, the effect of long-cherished association with God-like thought. An ignoble and bestial character, by the same process, is the result of the continued harboring of groveling thoughts.

We are made or unmade by ourselves. By our thoughts, we forge the weapons by which we can destroy ourselves. Likewise, we also fashion the tools with which we build for ourselves heavenly mansions of joy and strength and peace. By the right choice and true application of thought, we ascend to the Divine Perfection; by the abuse and wrong application of thought, we descend below the level of the beast. Between these two extremes are all the grades of character. We are our own maker and master.

Of all the beautiful truths pertaining to the soul which have been restored and brought to light in this

age, none is more gladdening or fruitful of divine promise and confidence than this—that we are the masters of
thought, the molders of character, and the makers and
shapers of condition, environment, and destiny.

As a being of Power, Intelligence, and Love, and the
lord of our own thoughts, each of us holds the key to
every situation and contains within ourselves that transforming and regenerative agency by which we may
make ourselves what we will.

Each of us is always our own master, even in our
weakest and most abandoned state. However, in a state
of weakness and degradation, we become foolish masters and misgovern the "household." When we begin to
reflect upon our condition and to search diligently for
the Law upon which our being is established, we then
will become wise masters, directing our energies with
intelligence and fashioning our thoughts to fruitful
issues. Such is the conscious master, and we can only
thus become by discovering within ourselves the laws of
thought—which discovery is totally a matter of application, self-analysis, and experience.

Only by such searching and mining are gold and dia-
monds obtained, and we can find every truth connected
with our being if we will dig deep into the mine of our
soul; and that we are the maker of our own character,

the molder of our own life, and the builder of our own destiny, we may unerringly prove, if we will watch, control, and alter our thoughts, tracing their effects upon ourselves, upon others, and upon our life and circumstances. By linking cause and effect, by patient practice and investigation, and utilizing every experience, even the most trivial everyday occurrence, we will obtain that knowledge of ourselves which is Understanding, Wisdom, and Power. In this direction, as in no other, is the law absolute: that we will find what we seek for, only by patience, practice, and ceaseless importunity. In this way can we enter the door of the Temple of Knowledge.

EFFECT OF THOUGHT ON CIRCUMSTANCES

The human mind may be likened to a garden, which may be intelligently cultivated or allowed to run wild. But whether cultivated or neglected, it must and will *bring forth*. If no useful seeds are put into it, then an abundance of useless weed-seeds will *fall,* accumulate, and will reproduce their own kind.

Just as the gardener cultivates the plot, keeping it free from weeds and cultivating the flowers and fruits which are required, so may we tend the garden of our mind, weeding out all the wrong, useless, and impure thoughts and cultivating toward perfection the flowers and fruits of right, useful, and pure thoughts.

By pursuing this process, we sooner or later discover that we are the master-gardener of our souls, the director of our lives. This lesson also reveals within ourselves the laws of thought and enables us to understand, with ever-increasing accuracy, how the thought-forces and mind elements operate in the shaping of our character, circumstances, and destiny.

Thought and character are one, and as character can manifest and discover itself only through environment and circumstance, the outer conditions of our life will always be found to be harmoniously related to our inner state. This does not mean that our circumstances at any given time are an indication of our entire character but that those circumstances are so intimately connected with some vital thought-element within ourselves that, for the time being, they are indispensable to our development.

Each of us is where we are by the law of our being. The thoughts which we have built into our character have brought us there. In the arrangement of our life there is no element of chance, but all is the result of a law which cannot err. This is just as true of those who feel "out of harmony" with their surroundings as of those who are contented with them.

As progressive and evolving beings, we are where we are that we may learn that we may grow. And as we learn the spiritual lesson, which any circumstance contains for us, it passes away and gives place to other circumstances.

We are buffeted by circumstances so long as we believe ourselves to be the creature of outside conditions; but when we realize that we are a creative power and that we may command the hidden soil and seeds of our being out of which circumstances arise, we then become the rightful masters of ourselves.

That circumstances *grow* out of thought, each of us, who has for any length of time practiced self-control and self-purification, knows—for we will have noticed that the alteration in our circumstances has been in exact ratio with our altered mental condition. So true is this that when we earnestly apply ourselves to remedy the defects in our character and make swift and marked progress, we pass rapidly through a succession of vicissitudes.

The soul attracts that which it secretly harbors, that which it loves, and also that which it fears; it reaches the height of its cherished aspirations; it falls to the level of its basest desires—and circumstances are the means by which the soul receives its own.

Every thought-seed sown or allowed to fall into the mind and to take root there produces its own, blossoming sooner or later into action and bearing its own harvest of opportunity and circumstance. Good thoughts bear good fruit, bad thoughts bad fruit.

The outer world of circumstance shapes itself to the inner world of thought, and both pleasant and unpleasant external conditions are factors which make for the ultimate good of the individual. As the reaper of our own harvest, we learn both by suffering and bliss.

Following the inmost desires, aspirations, thoughts by which we allow ourselves to be dominated (pursuing the frivolities of impure imaginings or steadfastly walking the highway of strong and high endeavor), we at last arrive at their fruition and fulfillment in the outer conditions of our lives. The laws of growth and adjustment are naturally followed.

One does not come to drunkenness or crime by the tyranny of fate or circumstance but by the pathway of groveling thoughts and base desires. Nor does a pure-minded person fall suddenly into crime by stress of any mere external force; the criminal thought had long been secretly fostered in the heart, and the hour of opportunity revealed its gathered power. No such conditions can exist as descending into vice and its attendant sufferings apart from vicious inclinations, or ascending into virtue and its pure happiness without the continued cultivation of virtuous aspirations. Therefore, as the lord and master of thoughts, we are the makers of ourselves, the shaper and author of our environment. Even at birth the soul comes to its own, and through every step of its earthly pilgrimage it attracts those combinations of conditions which reveal itself, which are the reflections of its own purity and impurity, its strength and weakness.

We do not attract that which we *want* but that which we *are*. Our whims, fancies, and ambitions are thwarted at every step, but our inmost thoughts and desires are fed with our own food, be it foul or clean. The "divinity that shapes our ends" is in ourselves; it is our very self. We are manacled only by ourselves: thought and action are the jailers of Fate—they imprison, being base; they are also the angels of Freedom—they liberate, being noble. Not what we wish and pray for do we get but what we justly earn. Our wishes and prayers are gratified and answered only when they harmonize with our thoughts and actions.

In the light of truth, what, then, is the meaning of "fighting against circumstances"? It means that we are continually revolting against an effect without, while all the time we are nourishing and preserving its cause in our heart. That cause may take the form of a conscious vice or an unconscious weakness; but whatever it is, it stubbornly impedes the efforts of its possessor, and hence calls aloud for remedy.

All of us are anxious to improve our circumstances but are unwilling to improve ourselves. We therefore remain bound. People who do not shrink from self-crucifixion can never fail to accomplish the object upon which their hearts are set. This is true of earthly as of heavenly things. Even those whose sole object is to acquire wealth must be prepared to make great personal sacrifices before they can accomplish this object; and how much more so for those people who would realize a strong and well-poised life?

For example, let's look at a man who is wretchedly poor. He is extremely anxious that his surroundings and home comforts should be improved, yet all the time he shirks his work and believes himself justified in trying to deceive his employer on the ground of the insufficiency of his wages. Such a man does not understand the simplest rudiments of these principles which are the basis of true prosperity, and is not only totally unfitted to rise out of his wretchedness but is actually attracting to himself a still deeper wretchedness by dwelling in, and acting out, indolent, deceptive, and negative thoughts.

Now let's look at a rich woman who is the victim of

a painful and persistent disease as a result of gluttony. She is willing to give large sums of money to get rid of it but will not sacrifice her gluttonous desires. She wants to gratify her taste for rich and unnatural foods and have her health as well. Such a woman is totally unfit to have health because she has not yet learned the first principles of a healthy life.

Another example is an employer of labor who adopts crooked measures to avoid paying the regulation wage and, in the hope of making larger profits, cuts the wages of his employees. Such a man is altogether unfitted for prosperity, and when he finds himself bankrupt, both as regards to reputation and riches, he blames circumstances, not knowing that he is the sole author of his condition.

I have introduced these three cases merely as illustrative of the truth that each person is the causer (though nearly always unconsciously) of his or her circumstances and that, while perhaps aiming at a good end, that person is continually frustrating its accomplishment by encouraging thoughts and desires which cannot possibly harmonize with that end. Such cases could be multiplied and varied almost indefinitely, but this is not necessary, as you can trace the action of the laws of thought in your own mind and life, and until this is done, mere external facts cannot serve as a ground of reasoning.

Circumstances, however, are so complicated, thought so deeply rooted, and the conditions of happiness vary so vastly with individuals that a person's entire soul-condition cannot be judged by another from the external aspects of his or her life alone. A person may he honest in certain directions, yet suffer privations; another may be dishonest in certain directions, yet acquire wealth. The usual conclusion, however, is that the one person fails *because of his or her particular honesty* and that the other prospers *because of that person's particular dishonesty.* This is the result of a superficial judgment, which assumes that the dishonest person is almost totally corrupt and the honest one almost entirely virtuous. In the light of a deeper knowledge and wider experience, such judgment is found to be erroneous. The dishonest person may have some admirable virtues, which the other does not possess; and the honest person obnoxious vices, which are absent in the other. The honest person reaps the good results of honest thoughts and acts but also is the cause of the sufferings, which his or her vices produce. The dishonest person likewise garners suffering and happiness.

It is pleasing to human vanity to believe that people suffer because of their virtues; but not until every sickly, bitter, and impure thought has been extirpated from their minds and every sinful stain washed from their souls can they be in a position to know and declare that the sufferings are the result of their good and not of their bad qualities. On the way to, yet long before that supreme perfection has been reached, such people will have experienced the Great Law which is absolutely just, and which cannot therefore give good for evil, evil for good. Possessed of such knowledge, they will then know, looking back upon their past ignorance and blindness, that each of their lives is and always was, justly ordered, and that all their past experiences, good and bad, were the equitable outworking of this evolving yet unevolved self.

Good thoughts and actions can never produce bad results; bad thoughts and actions can never produce good results. This is but saying that nothing can come from corn but corn, nothing from nettles but nettles. We understand this law in the natural world and work with it; but few understand it in the mental and moral world (though its operation there is just as simple and undeviating), and they therefore do not cooperate with it.

Suffering is *always* the effect of wrong thought in some direction. It is an indication that we are out of harmony with ourselves, with the Law of Life. The sole and supreme use of suffering is to purify, to burn out all that is useless and impure. Suffering ceases for those who are pure. There could be no object in burning gold after the dross had been removed, and a perfectly pure and enlightened being could not suffer.

The circumstances we encounter with suffering are the result of our own lack of mental harmony. The circumstances we encounter with blessedness are the result of our own mental harmony. Blessedness, not material possessions, is the measure of right thought; wretchedness, not lack of material possessions, is the measure of wrong thought. We may be cursed and rich; we may be blessed and poor. Blessedness and riches are joined together only when the riches are rightly and wisely used; and the poor person descends into wretchedness only when his or her lot is regarded as a burden unjustly imposed.

Indigence and indulgence are the two extremes of wretchedness. They are both equally unnatural and the result of mental disorder. We are not rightly conditioned until we are happy, healthy, and prosperous. Happiness, health, and prosperity are the result of a harmonious adjustment of the inner with the outer, of our relationship with our surroundings.

We begin to be mature adults only when we cease to whine and revile and commence to search for the hidden justice which regulates our lives. As we adapt our minds to that regulating factor, we cease to name others as the cause of our condition but begin to build ourselves up in strong and noble thoughts. We cease to kick against circumstances but begin to use them as aids to more rapid progress and as a means of discovering the hidden powers and possibilities within ourselves.

Law, not confusion, is the dominating principle in the universe; justice, not injustice, is the soul and substance of life; and righteousness, not corruption, is the molding and moving force in the spiritual government of the world. This being so, we must right ourselves to find that the universe is right; and during the process of putting ourselves right, we will find that as our thoughts are altered toward things and other people, things and other people will alter their thoughts toward us.

The proof of this truth is in every person, and it therefore admits of easy investigation by systematic introspection and self-analysis. Let us radically alter our thoughts, and we will be astonished at the rapid transformation it will effect in the material conditions of our lives. We may imagine that thought can be kept secret, but it cannot; it rapidly crystallizes into habit, and habit solidifies into circumstance. Bestial thoughts crystallize into habits of intoxication and consumption, which solidify into circumstances of destitution and disease. Impure thoughts of every kind crystallize into enervating and confusing habits, which solidify into distracting and adverse circumstances. Thoughts of fear, doubt, and indecision crystallize into weak, soft, and irresolute habits, which solidify into circumstances of failure, indigence, and slavish dependence. Lazy thoughts crystallize into habits of unseemliness and dishonesty, which solidify into circumstances of foulness and beggary. Hateful and condemnatory thoughts crystallize into habits of accusation and violence, which solidify into circumstances of injury and persecution. Selfish thoughts of all kinds crystallize into habits of self-seeking, which solidify into circumstances more or less distressing. On the other hand, beautiful thoughts of all kinds crystallize into habits of grace and kindliness, which solidify into genial and sunny circumstances. Pure thoughts crystallize into habits of temperance and self-control, which solidify into circumstances of repose and peace. Thoughts of courage, self-reliance, and decision crystallize into strong habits, which solidify into circumstances of success, plenty, and freedom. Energetic thoughts crystallize into habits of cleanliness and industry, which solidify into circumstances of pleasantness. Gentle and forgiving thoughts crystallize into habits of gentleness, which solidify into protective and preservative circumstances. Loving and unselfish thoughts crystallize into habits of self-forgetfulness for others, which solidify into circumstances of sure and abiding prosperity and true riches.

A particular train of thought persisted in, whether it is good or bad, cannot fail to produce its results on the character and circumstances. We cannot directly choose our circumstances, but we can choose our thoughts and so, indirectly yet surely, shape our circumstances.

Nature helps us to the gratification of encouraging thoughts, and opportunities are presented which will most speedily bring to the surface both the good and evil thoughts.

Let us cease from our sinful thoughts, and all the world will soften toward us and be ready to help us. Put away weak and sickly thoughts, and opportunities will spring up on every hand to aid our strong resolves. Encourage good thoughts, and no hard fate will drag us down to wretchedness and shame. The world is our kaleidoscope, and the varying combinations of colors, which at every succeeding moment it presents to us, are the exquisitely adjusted pictures of our ever-moving thoughts.

You will be what you will to be;
    Let failure find its false content
    In that poor world, "environment,"
But spirit scorns it, and is free.

It masters time, it conquers space,
    It cows that boastful trickster Chance,
    And bids the tyrant Circumstance
Uncrown and fill a servant's place.

The human Will, that force unseen,
    The offspring of a deathless Soul,
    Can hew a way to any goal,
Though walls of granite intervene.

Be not impatient in delay,
    But wait as one who understands;
    When spirit rises and commands,
The gods are ready to obey.

—ELLA WHEELER WILCOX

EFFECT OF THOUGHT ON
HEALTH AND BODY

The body is the servant of the mind. It obeys the operations of the mind, whether they be deliberately chosen or automatically expressed. At the bidding of unlawful thoughts the body sinks rapidly into disease and decay; at the command of glad and beautiful thoughts it becomes clothed with youthfulness and beauty.

Disease and health, like circumstances, are rooted in thought. Sickly thoughts will express themselves through a sickly body. Thoughts of fear have been known to kill a person as speedily as a bullet, and they are continually killing thousands of people just as surely though less rapidly. The people who live in fear of disease are the people who get it. Anxiety quickly demoralizes the whole body and lays it open to the entrance of disease; while impure thoughts, even if not physically indulged, will soon shatter the nervous system.

Strong, pure, and happy thoughts build up the body in vigor and grace. The body is a delicate and plastic instrument, which responds readily to the thoughts by which it is impressed, and habits of thought will produce their own effects, good or bad, upon it.

People will continue to have impure and poisoned blood so long as they propagate unclean thoughts. Out of a clean heart comes a clean life and a clean body. Out of a defiled mind proceeds a defiled life and a corrupt body. Thought is the font of action, life, and manifestation; make the fountain pure, and all will be pure.

Change of diet will not help us if we will not change our thoughts. When thoughts are made pure, impure food is no longer desired.

Clean thoughts make clean habits. The so-called saints who do not wash their bodies are not saints. Only when we have strengthened and purified our thoughts may the malevolent microbe not be considered.

If you would perfect your body, guard your mind. If you would renew your body, beautify your mind. Thoughts of malice, envy, disappointment, despondency, rob the body of its health and grace. A sour face does not come by chance; it is made by sour thoughts. Wrinkles that mar are drawn by folly, passion, and pride.

I know a woman of ninety-six who has the bright, innocent face of a girl. I know a man well under middle age whose face is drawn into inharmonious contours. The one is the result of a sweet and sunny disposition; the other is the outcome of passion and discontent.

As you cannot have a sweet and wholesome abode unless you admit the air and sunshine freely into your rooms, so a strong body and a bright, happy, or serene countenance can only result from the free admittance into the mind of thoughts of joy and goodwill and serenity.

On the faces of the aged there are wrinkles made by sympathy, others by strong and pure thought, and others are carved by passion: Who cannot distinguish them? With those who have lived righteously, age is calm, peaceful, and softly mellowed, like the setting sun. I have seen a philosopher on his deathbed. He was not old except in years. He died as sweetly and peacefully as he had lived.

There is no physician like cheerful thought for dissipating the ills of the body; there is no comforter to compare with goodwill for dispersing the shadows of grief and sorrow. To live continually in thoughts of ill will, cynicism, suspicion, and envy is to be confined in a self-made prison hole. But to think well of all, to be cheerful with all, to patiently learn to find the good in all—such unselfish thoughts are the very portals of heaven; and to dwell day by day in thoughts of peace toward every creature will bring abounding peace to their possessor.

THOUGHT AND PURPOSE

Until thought is linked with purpose, there is no intelligent accomplishment. With the majority, the ship of thought is allowed to "drift" upon the ocean of life. Aimlessness is a vice, and such drifting must not continue for those who would steer clear of catastrophe and destruction.

They who have no central purpose in their life fall an easy prey to petty worries, fears, troubles, and self-pitying, all of which are indications of weakness, which lead just as surely as deliberately planned sins (though by a different route) to failure, unhappiness, and loss. For weakness cannot persist in a power-evolving universe.

We should conceive of a legitimate purpose in our hearts and set out to accomplish it. We should make this purpose the centralizing point of our thoughts. It may take the form of a spiritual ideal or it may be a worldly object, according to our nature at the time. But whichever it is, we should steadily focus our thought forces upon the object, which we have set before us. We should make this purpose our supreme duty and should devote ourselves to its attainment, not allowing our thoughts to wander away into ephemeral fancies, long- ings, and imaginings. This is the royal road to self- control and true concentration of thought. Even if we fail again and again to accomplish our purpose (as we necessarily must until weakness is overcome), the *strength of character gained* will be the measure of our *true* success, and this will form a new starting-point for future power and triumph.

Those who are unprepared for the comprehension of a *great* purpose should fix their thoughts upon the fault- less performance of their duty, no matter how insignifi- cant their task may appear. Only in this way can the thoughts be gathered and focused and resolution and energy be developed, through which there is nothing that may not be accomplished.

The weakest soul, knowing its own weakness and believing this truth—*that strength can only be developed by effort and practice*—will, thus believing, at once begin to exert itself and, adding effort to effort, patience to patience, and strength to strength, will never cease to develop and will at last grow divinely strong.

As physically weak people can make themselves strong by careful and patient training, so people of weak thoughts can make their thoughts strong by exercising themselves in right thinking.

To put away aimlessness and weakness and to begin to think with purpose is to enter the ranks of those strong ones who recognize failure only as one of the pathways to attainment, who make all conditions serve them, and who think strongly, attempt fearlessly, and accomplish masterfully.

Having conceived of our purpose, we should mentally make out a *straight* pathway to its achievement, looking neither to the right nor the left. Doubts and fears should be rigorously excluded; they are disintegrating elements which break up the straight line of effort, rendering it crooked, ineffectual, useless. Thoughts of doubt and fear never accomplish anything and never can. They always lead to failure. Purpose, energy, power to do, and all strong thoughts cease when doubt and fear creep in.

The will to do springs from the knowledge that we can do. Doubt and fear are the great enemies of knowledge, and those who encourage them, who do not slay them, thwart themselves at every step.

When we have conquered doubt and fear, we have conquered failure. Our very thoughts are alive with power and all difficulties are bravely met and wisely overcome. Our purposes are seasonably planted, and they bloom and bring forth fruit that does not fall prematurely to the ground.

Thought allied fearlessly to purpose becomes creative force. Once we *know and accept this,* we are ready to become something higher and stronger than a mere bundle of wavering thoughts and fluctuating sensations. Once we apply this in our lives, we become the conscious and intelligent wielder of our mental powers.

THE THOUGHT-FACTOR
IN ACHIEVEMENT

All that we achieve and all that we fail to achieve is the direct result of our own thoughts. In a justly ordered universe, where loss of equipoise would mean total destruction, individual responsibility must be absolute. Our weakness and strength, purity and impurity, are our own and not another's. They are brought about by ourselves and not by others; and they can be altered only by ourselves, never by others. Our condition is also our own and not another's. Our suffering and our happiness are evolved from within. As we think, so we are; as we continue to think, so we remain.

A strong person cannot help a weaker unless that weaker is *willing* to be helped, and even then the weak must become strong by themselves. They must, by their own efforts, develop the strength which they admire in others. They and they alone can alter their condition.

It has been usual to think and to say, "Many people are slaves because one is an oppressor; let us hate the oppressor." Now, however, there is amongst an increasing few a tendency to reverse this judgment and to say, "One person is an oppressor because many are slaves; let us despise the slaves." The truth is that oppressor and slave are cooperators in ignorance and, while seeming to afflict each other, are in reality afflicting themselves. A perfect knowledge perceives the action of law in the weakness of the oppressed and the misapplied power of the oppressor; a perfect love, seeing the suffering which both states entail, condemns neither; a perfect compassion embraces both oppressor and oppressed.

Those who have conquered weakness and have put away all selfish thoughts belong neither to oppressor nor oppressed. They are free.

We can only rise, conquer, and achieve by lifting up our thoughts. We can only remain weak, abject, and miserable by refusing to lift our thoughts.

Before we can achieve anything, even in worldly things we must lift our thoughts above slavish animal indulgence. We may not, in order to succeed, give up *all* bestiality and selfishness by any means; but a portion of it must, at least, be sacrificed. If our first thought is bestial indulgence, we can neither think clearly nor plan methodically; we cannot find and develop our latent resources and would fail in any undertaking. Unless we can strongly control our thoughts, we are not in a position to control affairs and to adopt serious responsibilities. We are not fit to act independently and stand alone but are limited only by the thoughts which we choose.

There can be no progress, no achievement, without sacrifice, and our worldly success will be in the measure that we sacrifice our confused animal thoughts and fix our mind on the development of our plans and the strengthening of our resolution and self-reliance. And the higher we lift our thoughts, the more upright and righteous we become, the greater will be our success, the more blessed and enduring will be our achievements.

The universe does not favor the greedy, the dishonest, the vicious, although on the mere surface it may sometimes appear to do so; it helps the honest, the magnanimous, and the virtuous. All the great teachers of the ages have declared this in varying forms, and to prove and know it we have but to persist in making ourselves more and more virtuous by lifting up our thoughts.

Intellectual achievements are the result of thought consecrated to the search for knowledge or for the beautiful and true in life and nature. Such achievements may sometimes be connected with vanity and ambition, but they are not the outcome of those characteristics; they are the natural outgrowth of long and arduous effort and of pure and unselfish thoughts.

Spiritual achievements are the consummation of holy aspirations. Those who live constantly in the conception of noble and lofty thoughts, who dwell upon all that is pure and unselfish, will, as surely as the sun reaches its zenith and the moon its full, become wise and noble in character and rise into positions of influence and blessedness.

Achievement, of whatever kind, is the crown of effort, the diadem of thought. By the aid of self-control, resolution, purity, righteousness, and well-directed thought we ascend; by the aid of bestiality, indolence, impurity, corruption, and confusion of thought we descend.

People may rise to high success in the world and even to lofty altitudes in the spiritual realm and again descend into weakness and wretchedness by allowing arrogant, selfish, and corrupt thoughts to take possession of them.

Victories attained by right thought can only be

maintained by watchfulness. Many give way when success is assured and rapidly fall back into failure.

All achievements, whether in the business, intellectual, or spiritual world, are the result of definitely directed thought, are governed by the same law, and are of the same method; the only difference lies in the *object of attainment*.

They who would accomplish little must sacrifice little; they who would achieve much must sacrifice much; they who would attain highly must sacrifice greatly.

VISIONS AND IDEALS

The dreamers are the saviors of the world. As the visible world is sustained by the invisible, so we, through all our trials and sins and sordid vocations, are nourished by the beautiful visions of our solitary dreamers. Humanity cannot forget its dreamers; it cannot let their ideals fade and die; it lives in them; it knows them as the realities which it shall one day see and know.

Composer, sculptor, painter, poet, prophet, sage, these are the makers of the afterworld, the architects of heaven. The world is beautiful because they have lived; without them, laboring humanity would perish.

Those who cherish a beautiful vision, a lofty ideal in their hearts, will one day realize it. Columbus cherished a vision of another world, and he discovered it; Copernicus fostered the vision of a multiplicity of worlds and a wider universe, and he revealed it; Buddha beheld the vision of a spiritual world of stainless beauty and perfect peace, and he entered into it.

Cherish your visions; cherish your ideals; cherish the music that stirs in your heart, the beauty that forms in your mind, the loveliness that drapes your purest thoughts, for out of them will grow all delightful conditions, all heavenly environment; of these, if you but remain true to them, your world will at last be built.

To desire is to obtain; to aspire is to achieve. Shall our basest desires receive the fullest measure of gratification and our purest aspirations starve for lack of sustenance? Such is not the law; such a condition of things can never obtain: "Ask and receive."

Dream lofty dreams, and as you dream, so shall you become. Your vision is the promise of what you shall one day be; your ideal is the prophecy of what you shall at last unveil.

The greatest achievement was at first and for a time a dream. The oak sleeps in the acorn; the bird waits in the egg; and in the highest vision of the soul a waking angel stirs. Dreams are the seedlings of realities.

Your circumstances may be uncongenial, but they shall not long remain so if you but perceive an ideal and strive to reach it. You cannot travel *within* and stand still *without*. Think of a youth hard-pressed by poverty and labor, confined long hours in an unhealthy workshop, unschooled, and lacking all the arts of refinement. But he dreams of better things; he thinks of intelligence, of refinement, of grace and beauty. He conceives of, mentally builds up, an ideal condition of life; the vision of a wider liberty and a larger scope takes possession of him; unrest urges him to action, and he utilizes all his spare time and means, small though they are, to the development of his latent powers and resources. Very soon so altered has his mind become that the workshop can no longer hold him. It has become so out of harmony with his mentality that it falls out of his life as a garment is cast aside, and with the growth of opportunities, which fit the scope of his expanding powers, he passes out of it forever. Years later we see this youth as a full-grown man. We find him a master of certain forces of the mind, which he wields with worldwide influence and almost unequaled power. In his hands he holds the cords of gigantic responsibilities; he speaks, and lives are changed; men and women hang upon his words and remold their characters, and, sunlike, he becomes the fixed and luminous center round which innumerable destinies revolve. He has realized the vision of his youth. He has become one with his ideal.

And you too will realize the vision (not the idle wish) of your heart, be it base or beautiful, or a mixture of both, for you will always gravitate toward that which you secretly most love. Into your hands will be placed the exact results of your own thoughts; you will receive that which you earn—no more, no less. Whatever your present environment may be, you will fall, remain, or rise with your thoughts, your vision, your ideal. You will become as small as your controlling desire, as great as your dominant aspiration.

In the beautiful words of Stanton Kirkham Davis, "You may be keeping accounts, and presently you shall walk out of the door that for so long has seemed to you the barrier of your ideals, and shall find yourself before an audience—the pen still behind your ear, the ink stains on your fingers—and then and there shall pour out the torrent of your inspiration. You may be driving sheep, and you shall wander to the city—bucolic and open-mouthed; shall wander under the intrepid guidance of the spirit into the studio of a great master. After a time this master shall say, 'I have nothing more to teach you.'

And now you have become the master, who did so recently dream of great things while driving sheep. You shall lay down the saw and the plane to take upon yourself the regeneration of the world."

The thoughtless, the ignorant, and the indolent, seeing only the apparent effects of things and not the things themselves, talk of luck, of fortune, and of chance. Seeing others grow rich, they say, "How lucky they are!" Observing others become intellectual, they exclaim, "How highly favored they are!" And noting the saintly character and wide influence of still others, they remark, "How chance aids them at every turn!" They do not see the trials and failures and struggles which these people have voluntarily encountered in order to gain their experience; have no knowledge of the sacrifices they have made, of the undaunted efforts they have put forth, of the faith they have exercised, that they might overcome the apparently insurmountable and realize the vision of their heart. They do not know the darkness and the heartaches; they only see the light and joy and call it "luck," They do not see the long and arduous journey but only behold the pleasant goal and call it "good fortune." They do not understand the process but only perceive the result and call it "chance."

In all human affairs there are *efforts* and there are

results, and the strength of effort is the measure of the result. This is not mere chance. "Gifts," powers, material, intellectual, and spiritual possessions are the fruits of effort. They are thoughts completed, objects accomplished, visions realized.

The vision that you glorify in your mind, the ideal that you enthrone in your heart—this you will build your life by, this you will become.

SERENITY

Calmness of mind is one of the beautiful jewels of wisdom. It is the result of long and patient effort in self-control. Its presence is an indication of ripened experience, and of a more than ordinary knowledge of the laws and operations of thought.

We become calm in the measure that we understand ourselves as thought-evolved beings, for such knowledge necessitates the understanding of others as the result of thought, and as we develop a right understanding and see more and more clearly the internal relations of things by the action of cause and effect, we cease to fuss and fume and worry and grieve, and remain poised, steadfast, serene.

Calm people, having learned how to govern themselves, know how to adapt themselves to others; and they, in turn, reverence their spiritual strength and feel that they can learn from them and rely upon them. The more tranquil we become, the greater is our success, our influence, and our power for good. Even ordinary merchants will find business prosperity increase as they develop a greater self-control and equanimity, for people will always prefer to deal with people whose demeanor is strongly equable.

Strong, calm people are always loved and revered. They are like a shade-giving tree in a thirsty land or a sheltering rock in a storm. Who does not love a tranquil heart, a sweet-tempered balanced life? It does not matter whether it rains or shines or what changes come to those possessing these blessings, for they are always sweet, serene, and calm. That exquisite poise of character, which we call serenity, is the last lesson of culture; it is the flower of life, the fruit of the soul. It is precious as wisdom. It is more to be desired than gold, more even than fine gold. How insignificant mere money seeking looks in comparison with a serene life—a life that dwells in the ocean of truth, beneath the waves, beyond the reach of tempests, in the eternal calm.

How many people we know who sour their lives, who ruin all that is sweet and beautiful by explosive tempers, who destroy their poise of character and make bad blood! It is a question whether the great majorities of people do not ruin their lives and mar their happiness by lack of self-control. How few people we meet in life who are well balanced, who have that exquisite poise which is characteristic of the finished character!

Yes, humanity surges with uncontrolled passion, is tumultuous with ungoverned grief, is blown about by anxiety and doubt. Only those whose thoughts are controlled and purified make the winds and the storms of the soul obey them.

Tempest-tossed souls, wherever you may be, under whatsoever conditions you may live, know this—in the ocean of life the isles of blessedness are smiling, and the sunny shore of your ideal awaits your coming. Keep your hand firmly upon the helm of thought. In the bark of your soul reclines the commanding Master; He does but sleep; wake Him. Self-control is strength. Right thought is mastery. Calmness is power. Say unto your heart, "Peace, be still!"

From
POVERTY
to POWER

Let Love's bright sunshine play upon your heart;
Come now unto your gladness, peace and rest.
Bid the dark shades of selfishness depart,
And now and evermore be truly blest.

Author's Foreword to Original Edition

I looked around upon the world and saw that it was shadowed by sorrow and scorched by the fierce fires of suffering. And I looked for the cause. I looked around but could not find it; I looked in books but could not find it; I looked within and found there both the cause and the self-made nature of that cause. I looked again, and deeper, and found the remedy. I found one law, the law of love; one life, the life of adjustment to that law; one truth, the truth of a conquered mind and a quiet and obedient heart. And I dreamed of writing a book which should help men and women, whether rich or poor, learned or unlearned, worldly or unworldly, to find within themselves the source of all success, all happiness, all accomplishment, all truth. And the dream remained with me and at last became substantial; and now I send it forth into the world on its mission of healing and blessedness, knowing that it cannot fail to reach the homes and hearts of those who are waiting and ready to receive it.

—JAMES ALLEN

CONTENTS

FROM POVERTY TO POWER

PART I

The PATH
of PROSPERITY

THE LESSON
OF EVIL

Unrest and pain and sorrow are the shadows of life. There is no heart in all the world that has not felt the sting of pain, no mind that has not been tossed upon the dark waters of trouble, no eye that has not wept the hot, blinding tears of unspeakable anguish. There is no household where the great destroyers, disease and death, have not entered, severing heart from heart and casting over all the dark pall of sorrow. In the strong and apparently indestructible meshes of evil all are more or less fast caught; and pain, unhappiness, and misfortune wait upon humankind.

With the object of escaping, or in some way mitigating this overshadowing gloom, men and women rush blindly into innumerable devices, pathways by which they fondly hope to enter into a happiness that will not pass away. Such are those who revel in sensual excitements; such are the exclusive aesthetes, who shut themselves out from the sorrows of the world and surround themselves with enervating luxuries; such are those who thirst for wealth or fame and subordinate all things to the achievement of that object; and such are those who seek consolation in the performance of religious rites.

And to all, the happiness sought seems to come, and the soul for a time is lulled into a sweet security and an intoxicating forgetfulness of the existence of evil; but the day of disease comes at last, or some great sorrow, temptation, or misfortune breaks suddenly in on the unfortified soul, and the fabric of its fancied happiness is torn to shreds.

So over the head of every personal joy hangs the Damoclean sword of pain, ready at any moment to fall and crush the soul of those who are unprotected by knowledge.

The child cries to be a man or woman; the man and woman sigh for the lost felicity of childhood. The poor chafe under the chains of poverty by which they are bound, and the rich often live in fear of poverty or scour the world in search of an elusive shadow they call happiness. Sometimes the soul feels that it has found a secure peace and happiness in adopting a certain religion, in embracing an intellectual philosophy, or in building up an intellectual or artistic ideal; but some overpowering temptation proves the religion to be inadequate or insufficient; the theoretical philosophy is found to be a useless prop; or in a moment the idealistic statue upon which the devotee has for years been laboring is shattered into fragments.

Is there, then, no way of escape from pain and sorrow? Are there no means by which the bonds of evil may be broken? Are permanent happiness, security, prosperity, and abiding peace just a foolish dream? No, there is a way, and I speak it with gladness, by which evil can be overcome. There is a process by which disease, poverty, or any adverse condition or circumstance can be put on one side never to return. There is a method by which a permanent prosperity can be secured, free from all fear of the return of adversity, and there is a practice by which unbroken and unending peace and bliss can be partaken of and realized. The beginning of the way that leads to this glorious realization is the acquisition of a right understanding of the nature of evil.

It is not sufficient to deny or ignore evil; it must be understood. It is not enough to pray to God to remove the evil; you must find out why it is there and what lesson it has for you. It is of no avail to fret and fume and chafe at the chains that bind you; you must know why and how you are bound. Therefore, you must get outside yourself and must begin to examine and understand yourself. You must cease to be a disobedient child in the school of experience and must begin to learn, with humility and patience, the lessons that are set for your edification and ultimate perfection. For evil, when rightly understood, is found to be not an unlimited power or principle in the universe but a passing phase of human experience, and it therefore becomes a teacher to those who are willing to learn. Evil is not an abstract something outside yourself; it is an experience in your own heart, and by patiently examining and rectifying your heart, you will gradually be led into the discovery of the origin and nature of evil, which will necessarily be followed by its complete eradication.

All evil is corrective and remedial and is therefore not permanent. It is rooted in ignorance—ignorance of the true nature and relation of things, and so long as we remain in that state of ignorance, we remain subject to evil. There is no evil in the universe which is not the result of ignorance and which would not, if we were ready and willing to learn its lesson, lead us to higher wisdom and then vanish away. But people remain in evil, and it does not pass away because they are not willing or prepared to learn the lesson that it came to teach them.

I knew a child who every night when its mother took it to bed cried to be allowed to play with the candle; and one night, when the mother was off guard for a moment, the child took hold of the candle; the inevitable result followed, and the child never wished to play with the candle again. By its one foolish act, it learned, and learned perfectly, the lesson of obedience and entered into the knowledge that fire burns. And this incident is a complete illustration of the nature, meaning, and ultimate result of all sin and evil. As the child suffered through its own ignorance of the real nature of fire, so older children suffer through their ignorance of the real nature of the things which they weep for and strive after and which harm them when they are secured, the only difference being that in the latter case the ignorance and evil are more deeply rooted and obscure.

Evil has always been symbolized by darkness, and good by light, and hidden within the symbol is contained the perfect interpretation, the reality; for just as light always floods the universe, and darkness is only a mere speck or shadow cast by a small body intercepting a few rays of the illimitable light, so the light of the

Supreme Good is the positive and life-giving power which floods the universe, and evil the insignificant shadow cast by the self that intercepts and shuts off the illuminating rays which strive for entrance. When night folds the world in its black impenetrable mantle, no matter how dense the darkness, it covers but the small space of half our little planet, while the whole universe is ablaze with living light, and every soul knows that it will awake in the light in the morning. Know, then, that when the dark night of sorrow, pain, or misfortune settles down upon your soul and you stumble along with weary and uncertain steps, that you are merely intercepting your own personal desires between yourself and the boundless light of joy and bliss, and the dark shadow that covers you is cast by none and nothing but yourself. And just as the darkness without is but a negative shadow, an unreality which comes from nowhere, goes to nowhere, and has no abiding dwelling place, so the darkness within is equally a negative shadow passing over the evolving and light-born soul.

But why pass through the darkness of evil at all? Because by ignorance you have chosen to do so, and because by doing so you may understand both good and evil and may more appreciate the light by having passed through the darkness. As evil is the direct outcome of ignorance, so, when the lessons of evil are fully learned, ignorance passes away and wisdom takes its place. But as a disobedient child refuses to learn its lessons at school, so it is possible to refuse to learn the lessons of experience and thus to remain in continual darkness and to suffer continually recurring punishments in the form of disease, disappointment, and sorrow. If you wish to shake yourself free of the evil which encompasses you, you must be willing and ready to learn and must be prepared to undergo that disciplinary process without which no grain of wisdom or abiding happiness and peace can be secured.

You may shut yourself up in a dark room and deny that the light exists, when it is everywhere without and darkness exists only in this little room. So you may shut out the light of truth, or you may begin to pull down the walls of prejudice, self-seeking, and error that you have built around yourself and so let in the glorious and omnipresent light.

By earnest self-examination, strive to realize and not merely hold as a theory that evil is a passing phase, a self-created shadow, that all your pains, sorrows, and misfortunes have come to you by a process of undeviating and absolutely perfect law; have come to you because you deserve and require them, and that by first enduring and then understanding them, you may be made stronger, wiser, nobler. When you have fully entered into this realization, you will be in a position to mold your own circumstances, to transmute all evil into good and to weave with a master hand the fabric of your destiny.

THE WORLD A REFLEX
OF MENTAL STATES

What you are, so is your world. Everything in the universe is resolved into your own inward experience. It matters little what is without, for it is all a reflection of your own state of consciousness. It matters everything what you are within, for everything without will be mirrored and colored accordingly.

All that you positively know is contained in your own experience; all that you ever will know must pass through the gateway of experience, and so become part of yourself.

Your own thoughts, desires, and aspirations comprise your world, and, to you, all that there is in the universe of beauty and joy and bliss, or of ugliness and sorrow and pain, are contained within yourself. By your own thoughts you make or mar your life, your world, your universe. As you build within by the power of thought, so will your outward life and circumstances shape themselves accordingly. Whatsoever you harbor in the inmost chambers of your heart will sooner or later, by the inevitable law of reaction, shape itself in your outward life. The soul that is impure, sordid, and selfish is gravitating with unerring precision toward misfortune and catastrophe; the soul that is pure, unselfish, and noble is gravitating with equal precision toward happiness and prosperity. Every soul attracts its own, and nothing can possibly come to it that does not belong to it. To realize this is to recognize the universality of divine law. The incidents of every human life, which both make and mar, are drawn to it by the quality and power of its own inner thought-life. Every soul is a complex combination of gathered experiences and thoughts, and the body is but an improvised vehicle for its manifestation. What, therefore, your thoughts are, that is your real self; and the world around, both animate and inanimate, wears the aspect with which your thoughts clothe it. "All that we are is the result of what we have thought; it is founded on our thoughts; it is made up of our thoughts." Thus said Buddha, and it therefore follows that if you are happy, it is because you dwell in happy thoughts; if miserable, because you dwell in despondent and debilitating thoughts. Whether one is fearful or fearless, foolish or wise, troubled or serene, within that soul lies the cause of its own state or states, and never without. And now I seem to hear a chorus of voices exclaim, "But do you really mean to say that outward circumstances do not affect our minds?" I do not say that, but I say this, and know it to be an infallible truth, that circumstances can only affect you insofar as you allow them to do so. You are swayed by circumstances because you have not a right understanding of the nature, use, and power of thought. You *believe* (and upon this little word "belief" hang all our sorrows and joys) that outward things have the power to make or mar your life; by so doing, you submit to those outward things, confess that you are their slave and they your unconditional master; by so doing, you invest them with a power which they do not, of themselves, possess, and you succumb, in reality, not to the mere circumstances but to the gloom or gladness, the fear or hope, the strength or weakness which your thought-sphere has thrown around them.

I knew two men who, at an early age, lost the hard-earned savings of years. One was very deeply troubled and gave way to chagrin, worry, and despondency. The other, on reading in his morning paper that the bank in which his money was deposited had hopelessly failed and that he had lost all, quietly and firmly remarked, "Well, it's gone, and trouble and worry won't bring it back, but hard work will." He went to work with renewed vigor and rapidly became prosperous, while the former man, continuing to mourn the loss of his money and to grumble at his "bad luck," remained the victim and tool of adverse circumstances, in reality of his own weak and slavish thoughts. The loss of money was a curse to the one because he clothed the event with dark and dreary thoughts; it was a blessing to the other because he threw around it thoughts of strength, of hope, and of renewed endeavor.

If circumstances had the power to bless or harm, they would bless and harm all people alike, but the fact that the same circumstances will be alike good and bad to different souls proves that the good or bad is not in the circumstance but only in the mind of those who encounter it. When you begin to realize this, you will begin to control your thoughts, to regulate and discipline your mind, and to rebuild the inward temple of your soul, eliminating all useless and superfluous material and incorporating into your being thoughts alone of joy and serenity, of strength and life, of compassion and love, of beauty and immortality; and as you do this, you will become joyful and serene, strong and healthy, compassionate and loving, and beautiful with the beauty of immortality.

And as we clothe events with the drapery of our own thoughts, so likewise do we clothe the objects of the visible world around us, and where one sees harmony and beauty, another sees revolting ugliness. An enthusiastic naturalist was one day roaming the country lanes in pursuit of his hobby and during his rambles came upon a pool of brackish water near a farmyard. As he proceeded to fill a small bottle with the water for the purpose of examination under the microscope, he proclaimed, with more enthusiasm than discretion, to an uncultivated farm boy who stood close by, upon the hidden and innumerable wonders contained in the pool, and concluded by saying, "Yes, my friend, within this pool is contained a hundred, nay, a million universes, had we but the sense or the instrument by which we could apprehend them." And the unsophisticated one ponderously remarked, "I know the water be full o' tadpoles, but they be easy to catch." Where the naturalist, whose mind was stored with the knowledge of natural facts, saw beauty, harmony, and hidden glory, the mind unenlightened upon those things saw only an offensive mud puddle.

The wildflower that the casual wayfarer thoughtlessly tramples upon is, to the spiritual eye of the poet, an angelic messenger from the invisible. To the many, the ocean is but a dreary expanse of water on which ships sail and are sometimes wrecked; to the soul of the musician it is a living thing, and she hears, in all its changing moods, divine harmonies. Where the ordinary mind sees disaster and confusion, the mind of the philosopher sees the most perfect sequence of cause and effect, and where the materialist sees nothing but endless death, the mystic sees pulsating and eternal life.

And as we clothe both events and objects with our own thoughts, so likewise do we clothe the souls of others in the garments of our thoughts. The suspicious believe everybody to be suspicious; liars feel secure in the thought that they are not so foolish as to believe that there is such a phenomenon as a strictly truthful person; the envious see envy in every soul; misers think everybody is eager to get their money. Those who have subordinated conscience in the making of their wealth sleep with a revolver under their pillow, wrapped in the delusion that the world is full of conscienceless people who are eager to rob them. The abandoned sensualist looks upon the saint as a hypocrite; on the other hand, those who dwell in loving thoughts see in all that which calls forth their love and sympathy. The trusting and honest are not troubled by suspicions; the good-natured and charitable who rejoice at the good fortune of others, scarcely know what envy means; and those who have realized the Divine within themselves recognize it in all beings, even in the beasts.

Men and women are confirmed in their mental outlook because of the fact that by the law of cause and effect, they attract to themselves that which they send forth and so come in contact with people similar to themselves. The old adage "Birds of a feather flock together" has a deeper significance than is generally attached to it, for in the thought-world as in the world of matter, each clings to its kind.

Do you wish for kindness? Be kind.
Do you ask for truth? Be true.
What you give of yourself you find;
Your world is a reflex of you.

If you are one of those who are praying for and looking forward to a happier world beyond the grave, here is a message of gladness for you: you may enter into and realize that happy world now; it fills the whole universe and it is within you, waiting for you to find, acknowledge, and possess. What you have to do is to believe this, simply believe it with a mind unclouded by doubt, and then meditate upon it till you understand it. You will then begin to purify and to build your inner world, and as you proceed, passing from revelation to revelation, from realization to realization, you will discover the utter powerlessness of outward things beside the magic potency of a self-governed soul.

THE WAY OUT OF
UNDESIRABLE CONDITIONS

Having seen and realized that evil is but a passing shadow thrown by the intercepting self across the transcendent form of the Eternal Good, and that the world is a mirror in which each of us sees a reflection of ourselves, we now ascend, by firm and easy steps, to that plane of perception where the vision of the law is seen and realized. With this realization comes the knowledge that everything is included in a ceaseless interaction of cause and effect and that nothing can possibly be divorced from law. From the most trivial thought, word, or act of humankind, up to the groupings of the celestial bodies, law reigns supreme. No arbitrary condition can, even for one moment, exist, for such a condition would be a denial and an annihilation of law. Every condition of life is, therefore, bound up in an orderly and harmonious sequence, and the secret and cause of every condition is contained within itself. The law "Whatsoever a man sows that shall he also reap" is inscribed in flaming letters upon the portal of Eternity, and none can deny it, none can cheat it, none can escape it. If you put your hand in the fire, you must suffer the burning until such time as it has worked itself out, and neither curses nor prayers can avail to alter it.

Precisely the same law governs the realm of mind. Hatred, anger, jealousy, envy, lust, covetousness, all these are fires which burn, and whoever even so much as touches them must suffer the torments of burning. All these conditions of mind are rightly called "evil," for they are the efforts of the soul to subvert, in its ignorance, the law, and they therefore lead to chaos and confusion within, and are sooner or later actualized in the outward circumstances as disease, failure, and misfortune, coupled with grief, pain, and despair. Whereas love, gentleness, goodwill, and purity are cooling airs which breathe peace upon the soul that woos them, and being in harmony with the eternal law, they become actualized in the form of health, peaceful surroundings, and undeviating success and good fortune.

A thorough understanding of this great law that permeates the universe leads to the acquisition of that state of mind known as *obedience*. To know that justice, harmony, and love are supreme in the universe is likewise to know that all adverse and painful conditions are the result of our own disobedience to that law. Such knowledge leads to strength and power, and it is upon such knowledge alone that a true life and an enduring success and happiness can be built. To be patient under all circumstances, and to accept all conditions as necessary factors in your training, is to rise superior to all painful conditions and to overcome them with an overcoming which is sure and which leaves no fear of their return, for by the power of obedience to law they are utterly slain. By obedience, you are working in harmony with the law, have identified with the law, and whatsoever you conquer you conquer forever; whatsoever you build can never be destroyed.

The cause of all power as of all weakness is within: the secret of all happiness as of all misery is likewise within. There is no progress apart from unfoldment within and no sure foothold of prosperity or peace except by orderly advancement in knowledge.

You say you are chained by circumstances; you cry out for better opportunities, for a wider scope, for improved physical conditions, and perhaps you inwardly curse the fate that binds you hand and foot. It is for you that I write; it is to you that I speak. Listen, and let my words burn themselves into your heart, for that which I say to you is truth: you may bring about that improved condition in your outward life which you desire if you will unswervingly resolve to improve your inner life. I know this pathway looks barren at its commencement (truth always does—it is only error and delusion which are at first inviting and fascinating), but if you undertake to walk it, if you perseveringly discipline your mind, eradicating your weaknesses and allowing your soul-forces and spiritual powers to unfold themselves, you will be astonished at the magical changes which will be brought about in your outward life. As you proceed, golden opportunities will be strewn across your path, and the power and judgment to properly utilize them will spring up within you. Genial friends will come unbidden to you; sympathetic souls will be drawn to you as the needle is to the magnet; and books and all outward aids that you require will come to you unsought.

Perhaps the chains of poverty hang heavily upon you, and you are friendless and alone, and you long with an intense longing that your load may be lightened; but the load continues, and you seem to be enveloped in an ever-increasing darkness. Perhaps you complain, you bewail your lot; you blame your birth, your parents, your employer, or the unjust powers who have bestowed upon you so undeservedly poverty and hardship, and upon another affluence and ease.

Cease your complaining and fretting; none of these things that you blame are the cause of your poverty; the cause is within yourself, and where the cause is, there is the remedy. The very fact that you are a complainer shows that you deserve your lot, shows that you lack that faith which is the ground of all effort and progress. There is no room for a complainer in a universe of law, and worry is soul-suicide. By your very attitude of mind you are strengthening the chains which bind you and are drawing about you the darkness by which you are enveloped. Alter your outlook upon life, and your outward life will alter.

Build yourself up in the faith and knowledge, and make yourself worthy of better surroundings and wider opportunities. Be sure, first of all, that you are making the best of what you have. Do not delude yourself into supposing that you can step into greater advantages while overlooking smaller ones, for if you could, the advantage would be impermanent and you would quickly fall back again in order to learn the lesson that you had neglected. As the child at school must master one standard before passing on to the next, so, before you can have that greater good which you so desire, you must faithfully employ that which you already possess.

Perhaps you are living in a small cottage and are surrounded by unhealthy and vicious influences. You desire a larger and more sanitary residence. Then you must fit yourself for such a residence by first of all making your cottage as far as possible a little paradise. Keep it spotlessly clean. Make it look as pretty and sweet as your limited means will allow. Cook your plain food with all care, and arrange your humble table as tastefully as you possibly can. If you cannot afford a carpet, let your rooms be carpeted with smiles and welcomes, fastened down with the nails of kind words driven in with the hammer of patience. Such a carpet will not fade in the sun, and constant use will never wear it away.

By so ennobling your present surroundings you will rise above them, and above the need of them, and at the right time you will pass on into the better house and surroundings which have all along been waiting for you and which you have fitted yourself to occupy.

Perhaps you desire more time for thought and effort and feel that your hours of labor are too hard and long. Then see to it that you are utilizing to the fullest possible extent what little spare time you have. It is useless to desire more time if you are already wasting what little you have, for you would only grow more indolent and indifferent.

Even poverty and lack of time and leisure are not the evils that you imagine they are, and if they hinder you in your progress, it is because you have clothed them in your own weaknesses, and the evil that you see in them is really in yourself. Endeavor to fully and completely realize that insofar as you shape and mold your mind, you are the maker of your destiny, and as by the transmuting power of self-discipline you realize this more and more, you will come to see that these so-called evils may be converted into blessings. You will then utilize your poverty for the cultivation of patience, hope, and courage; and your lack of time in the gaining of promptness of action and decision of mind, by seizing the precious moments as they present themselves for your acceptance. As in the rankest soil the most beautiful flowers are grown, so in the dark soil of poverty the choicest flowers of humanity have developed and bloomed.

Where there are difficulties to cope with and unsatisfactory conditions to overcome, there virtue most flourishes and manifests its glory.

It may be that you are in the employ of a tyrannical master or mistress, and you feel that you are harshly treated. Look upon this also as necessary to your training. Return your employer's unkindness with gentleness and forgiveness. Practice unceasingly patience and self-control. Turn the disadvantage to account by utilizing it for the gaining of mental and spiritual strength, and by your silent example and influence you will thus be teaching your employer, will be helping that person to grow ashamed of such conduct, and will, at the same time, be lifting yourself up to that height of spiritual attainment by which you will be enabled to step into new and more congenial surroundings at the time when they are presented to you. Do not complain that you are a slave but lift yourself up, by noble conduct, above the plane of slavery. Before complaining that you are a slave to another, be sure that you are not a slave to self. Look within; look searchingly and have no mercy upon yourself. You will find there, perchance, slavish thoughts, slavish desires, and in your daily life and conduct slavish habits. Conquer these; cease to be a slave to self, and no one will have the power to enslave you. As you overcome self, you will overcome all adverse conditions, and every difficulty will fall before you.

Do not complain that the rich oppress you. Are you

sure that if you gained riches you would not be an oppressor yourself? Remember that there is the eternal law which is absolutely just, and that those who oppress today must themselves be oppressed tomorrow; and from this there is no way of escape. And perhaps yesterday you were rich and an oppressor, and that now you are merely paying off the debt that you owe to the great law. Practice, therefore, fortitude and faith. Dwell constantly in mind upon the eternal justice, the eternal good. Endeavor to lift yourself above the personal and the transitory into the impersonal and permanent. Shake off the delusion that you are being injured or oppressed by another, and try to realize, by a profounder comprehension of your inner life and the laws that govern that life, that you are only really injured by what is within you.

There is no practice more degrading, debasing, and soul-destroying than that of self-pity. Cast it out from you. While such a canker is feeding upon your heart, you can never expect to grow into a fuller life. Cease from the condemnation of others, and begin to condemn yourself. Condone none of your acts, desires, or thoughts that will not bear comparison with spotless purity or endure the light of sinless good. By so doing, you will be building your house upon the rock of the

Eternal, and all that is required for your happiness and well-being will come to you in its own time.

There is positively no way of permanently rising above poverty or any undesirable condition except by eradicating those selfish and negative conditions within, of which these are the reflection and by virtue of which they continue. The way to true riches is to enrich the soul by the acquisition of virtue. Outside of real heart-virtue, there is neither prosperity nor power but only the appearances of these. I am aware that people make money who have acquired no measure of virtue and have little desire to do so; but such money does not constitute true riches, and its possession is transitory and feverish.

Here is King David's testimony:

For I was envious at the foolish, when I saw the prosperity of the wicked. . . . Their eyes stand out with fatness; they have more than heart could wish. . . . Verily I have cleansed my heart in vain, and washed my hands in innocence. . . . When I thought to know this, it was too painful for me; until I went into the sanctuary of God; then understood I their end.

The prosperity of the wicked was a great trial to David until he went into the sanctuary of God, and then

he knew their end. You likewise may go into that sanctuary. It is within you. It is that state of consciousness
that remains when all that is sordid, personal, and
impermanent is risen above, and universal and eternal
principles are realized.

That is the God state of consciousness; it is the sanctuary of the Most High. When by long strife and self-
discipline, you have succeeded in entering the door of
that holy Temple, you will perceive, with unobstructed
vision, the end and fruit of all human thought and
endeavor, both good and evil. You will then no longer
relax your faith when you see immoral people accumulating outward riches, for you will know that they must
come again to poverty and degradation.

Rich people who are barren of virtue are, in reality,
poor, and as surely as the waters of the river are drifting
to the ocean, so surely is he, in the midst of all his riches,
drifting toward poverty and misfortune; and though
they die rich, yet must they return to reap the bitter fruit
of all of their immorality. And though they become rich
many times, yet as many times must they be thrown
back into poverty until by long experience and suffering
they conquer the poverty within. But those who are
outwardly poor yet rich in virtue are truly rich, and in
the midst of all their poverty, they are surely traveling

toward prosperity; and abounding joy and bliss await their coming.

If you would become truly and permanently prosperous, you must first become virtuous. It is therefore unwise to aim directly at prosperity, to make it the one object of life, to reach out greedily for it. To do this is to ultimately defeat yourself. But rather aim at self-perfection, make useful and unselfish service the object of your life, and ever reach out hands of faith toward the supreme and unalterable Good.

You say you desire wealth, not for your own sake but in order to do good with it and to bless others. If this is your real motive in desiring wealth, then wealth will come to you, for you are strong and unselfish indeed if in the midst of riches you are willing to look upon yourself as steward and not as owner. But examine well your motive, for in the majority of instances where money is desired for the admitted object of blessing others, the real underlying motive is a love of popularity and a desire to pose as a philanthropist or reformer. If you are not doing good with what little you have, depend upon it the more money you acquire the more selfish you would become, and all the good you appeared to do with your money, if you attempted to do any, would be so much insinuating self-laudation.

If your real desire is to do good, there is no need to wait for money before you do it; you can do it now, this very moment, and just where you are. If you are really so unselfish as you believe yourself to be, you will show it by sacrificing yourself for others now. No matter how poor you are, there is room for self-sacrifice. The heart that truly desires to do good does not wait for money before doing it but comes to the altar of sacrifice and, leaving there the unworthy elements of self, goes out and breathes upon neighbor and stranger, friend and enemy alike, the breath of blessedness.

As the effect is related to the cause, so are prosperity and power related to the inward good, and poverty and weakness to the inward evil. Money does not constitute true wealth, or position, or power, and to rely upon it alone is to stand upon a slippery place.

Your true wealth is your stock of virtue, and your true power the uses to which you put it. Rectify your heart and you will rectify your life. Lust, hatred, anger, vanity, pride, covetousness, self-indulgence, self-seeking, obstinacy—all these are poverty and weakness; whereas love, purity, gentleness, meekness, patience, compassion, generosity, self-forgetfulness, and self-renunciation—all these are wealth and power.

As the elements of poverty and weakness are overcome,

an irresistible and all-conquering power is evolved from within, and those who succeed in establishing themselves in the highest virtue bring the whole world to their feet.

But the rich, as well as the poor, have their undesirable conditions and are frequently further removed from happiness than the poor. And here we see how happiness depends not upon outward aids or possessions but upon the inward life. Perhaps you are an employer, and you have endless trouble with those whom you employ, and when you do get good and faithful employees, they quickly leave you. As a result, you are beginning to lose or have completely lost your faith in human nature. You try to remedy matters by giving better wages and by allowing certain liberties, yet matters remain unaltered. Let me advise you. The secret of all your trouble is not in your servants; it is in yourself. If you look within, with a humble and sincere desire to discover and eradicate your error, you will sooner or later find the origin of all your unhappiness. It may be some selfish desire, or lurking suspicion, or unkind attitude of mind that sends out its poison upon those about you and reacts upon yourself, even though you may not show it in your manner or speech.

Think of your employees with kindness, consider their happiness and comfort, and never demand of them that extremity of service that you yourself would not care to perform were you in their place. Rare and beautiful is that humility of soul by which workers entirely forge themselves in their employer's good; but far rarer, and beautiful with a divine beauty, is that nobility of soul by which people, forgetting their own happiness, seek the happiness of those who are under their authority and who depend upon them for their bodily sustenance. Such people's happiness is increased tenfold, and they do not need to complain about those whom they employ.

A well-known and extensive employer of labor said this about his success in keeping good employees: "I have always had the happiest relations with my workforce. If you ask me how it is to be accounted for, I can only say that it has been my aim from the first to do to them as I would wish to be done by." This is the secret by which all desirable conditions are secured, and all that are undesirable are overcome. Do you say that you are lonely and unloved and have not a friend in the world? Then, I pray you, for the sake of your own happiness, blame nobody but yourself. Be friendly toward others, and friends will soon flock round you. Make yourself pure and lovable, and you will be loved by all.

Whatever conditions are rendering your life burdensome, you may pass out of and beyond them by developing and utilizing within you the transforming power of self-purification and self-conquest. Whether it is the poverty which galls or the riches which burden, or the many misfortunes, griefs, and annoyances which form the dark background in the web of life, you may overcome them by overcoming the selfish elements within which give them life.

It matters not that by the unfailing law there are past thoughts and acts to work out and to atone for. By the same law, we are setting in motion, during every moment of our life, fresh thoughts and acts, and we have the power to make them good or ill. Nor does it follow that if people (reaping what they have sown) must lose money or forfeit position, that they must also lose their fortitude or forfeit their uprightness. It is in these that their wealth and power and happiness are to be found.

Those who cling to their self-centeredness are their own enemy, and they are surrounded by enemies. Those who relinquish their self-centeredness are their own saviors and are surrounded by friends like a protecting belt. Before the divine radiance of a pure heart all darkness vanishes and all clouds melt away, and those who have conquered their self-centeredness have conquered the universe.

Come, then, out of your poverty; come out of your pain; come out of your troubles, and sighs, and complaints, and heartaches, and loneliness by coming out of yourself. Let the old tattered garment of your petty self-centeredness fall from you, and put on the new garment of universal love. You will then realize the inward heaven, and it will be reflected in all your outward life.

Those who set their feet firmly upon the path of self-conquest, who walk, aided by the staff of faith, the highway of self-sacrifice, will assuredly achieve the highest prosperity and will reap abounding and enduring joy and bliss.

THE SILENT POWER OF
THOUGHT: CONTROLLING
AND DIRECTING ONE'S
FORCES

The most powerful forces in the universe are the silent forces; and in accordance with the intensity of its power does a force become beneficent when rightly directed and destructive when wrongly employed. This is a common knowledge in regard to the mechanical forces, such as steam, electricity, etc., but few have yet learned to apply this knowledge to the realm of mind, where the thought-forces (most powerful of all) are continually being generated and sent forth as currents of salvation or destruction.

At this stage of our evolution, we have entered into the possession of these forces, and the whole trend of our present advancement is their complete subjugation. All the wisdom possible to us on this material earth is to be found only in complete self-mastery, and the command "Love your enemies" resolves itself into an exhortation to enter here and now into the possession of that sublime wisdom by taking hold of, mastering, and transmuting those mind forces to which we are now slavishly subject and by which we are helplessly borne, like a straw on the stream, upon the currents of selfishness.

The Hebrew prophets, with their perfect knowledge of the Supreme Law, always related outward events to inward thought and associated national disaster or success with the thoughts and desires that dominated the nation at the time. The knowledge of the causal power of thought is the basis of all their prophecies, as it is the basis of all real wisdom and power. National events are simply the working out of the psychic forces of the nation. Wars, plagues, and famines are the meeting and clashing of wrongly directed thought-forces, the culminating points at which destruction steps in as the agent of the law. It is foolish to ascribe war to the influence of one person or to one body of people. It is the crowning horror of national selfishness.

It is the silent and conquering thought-forces that bring all things into manifestation. The universe grew out of thought. Matter in its last analysis is found to be merely objectified thought. All human accomplishments were first wrought out in thought and then materialized. Authors, inventors, and architects first build up their work in thought and, having perfected it in all its parts as a complete and harmonious whole upon the thought-plane, then commence to materialize it, to bring it down to the material or sense-plane.

When the thought-forces are directed in harmony ith the overruling Law, they are upbuilding and preservative, but when subverted they become disintegrating and self-destructive.

To adjust all your thoughts to a perfect and unswerving faith in the omnipotence and supremacy of good is to cooperate with that good and to realize within yourself the solution and destruction of all evil. Believe and you shall live. And here we have the true meaning of salvation: salvation from the darkness and negation of evil by entering into and realizing the living light of the Eternal Good.

Where there is fear, worry, anxiety, doubt, trouble, chagrin, or disappointment, there is ignorance and lack of faith. All these conditions of mind are the direct outcome of selfishness and are based upon an inherent belief in the power and supremacy of evil. They therefore constitute practical atheism; and to live in and become subject to these negative and soul-destroying conditions of mind is the only real atheism.

It is salvation from such conditions that humankind needs, and we cannot boast of salvation if we are their helpless and obedient slave. To fear or to worry is as sinful as to curse, for if we intrinsically *believe* in the eternal justice, the omnipotent good, the boundless love, there is no reason to fear or to worry. To fear, to worry, to doubt, is to deny, to disbelieve.

It is from such states of mind that all weakness and failure proceed, for they represent the annulling and disintegrating of the positive thought-forces which would otherwise speed to their object with power and bring about their own beneficent results.

To overcome these negative conditions is to enter into a life of power, is to cease to be a slave and to become a master, and there is only one way by which they can be overcome, and that is by steady and persistent growth in inward knowledge. To mentally deny evil is not sufficient; it must, by daily practice, be risen above and understood. To mentally affirm the good is inadequate; it must, by unswerving endeavor, be entered into and comprehended.

The intelligent practice of self-control quickly leads to a knowledge of one's interior thought-forces and, later on, to the acquisition of that power by which they are rightly employed and directed. In the measure that you master yourself, that you control your mental forces instead of being controlled by them, in just such measure will you master affairs and outward circumstances.

There are people under whose touch everything crumbles away and who cannot retain success even when it is placed in their hands. Such people dwell continually in those conditions of mind that are the very negation of power. To be forever wallowing in the bogs of doubt, to be drawn continually into the quicksand of fear, or blown ceaselessly about by the winds of anxiety is to be a slave and to live the life of a slave, even though success and influence be forever knocking at your door seeking for admittance. Such people, being without faith and without self-government are incapable of the right government of their affairs and are slaves to circumstances—in reality, slaves to themselves. Such are taught by affliction and ultimately pass from weakness to strength by the stress of bitter experience.

Faith and purpose constitute the motive power of life. There is nothing that a strong faith and an unflinching purpose may not accomplish. By the daily exercise of silent faith, the thought-forces are gathered together, and by the daily strengthening of silent purpose, those forces are directed toward the object of accomplishment.

Whatever your position in life may be, before you can hope to enter into any measure of success, usefulness, and power, you must learn how to focus your thought-forces by cultivating calmness and repose. It may be that you are a business executive and you are suddenly confronted with some overwhelming difficulty or probable disaster. You grow fearful and anxious and are at your wit's end. To persist in such a state of mind would be fatal, for when anxiety steps in, correct judgment passes out. Now if you will take advantage of a quiet hour or two in the early morning or at night and go away to some solitary spot, or to some room in your house where you know you will be absolutely free from intrusion, and having seated yourself in an easy attitude, you forcibly direct your mind right away from the object of anxiety by dwelling upon something in your life that is pleasing and bliss-giving, a calm, reposeful strength will gradually steal into your mind and your anxiety will pass away. Upon the instant that you find your mind reverting to the lower plane of worry, bring it back again and reestablish it on the plane of peace and strength. When this is fully accomplished, you may then concentrate your whole mind upon the solution of your difficulty, and what was intricate and insurmountable to you in your hour of anxiety will be made plain and easy, and you will see, with that clear vision and perfect judgment which belong only to a calm and untroubled mind, the right course to pursue and the proper end to be brought about. It may be that you will have to try day after day before you will be able to perfectly calm your mind, but if you persevere, you will certainly accomplish it, and the course that is presented to you in that hour of calmness must be carried out. Doubtless when you are again involved in the business of the day and worries again creep in and begin to dominate you, you will begin to think that the course is a wrong or foolish one, but do not heed such suggestions. Be guided absolutely and entirely by the vision of calmness and not by the shadows of anxiety. The hour of calmness is the hour of illumination and correct judgment. By such a course of mental discipline the scattered thought-forces are reunited and directed like the rays of the searchlight upon the problem at issue, with the result that it gives way before them.

There is no difficulty, however great, but that will yield before a calm and powerful concentration of thought, and no legitimate object may be but speedily actualized by the intelligent use and direction of one's soul-forces.

Not until you have gone deeply and searchingly into your inner nature, and have overcome many enemies that lurk there, can you have any approximate conception of the subtle power of thought, of its inseparable relation to outward and material things, or of its magical potency, when rightly poised and directed, in readjusting and transforming the life conditions.

Every thought you think is a force sent out, and in accordance with its nature and intensity will it go out to seek a lodgment in minds receptive to it and will react upon yourself for good or evil. There is ceaseless reciprocity between mind and mind and a continual interchange of thought-forces. Selfish and disturbing thoughts are so many malignant and destructive forces, messengers of evil, sent out to stimulate and augment the evil in other minds, which in turn send them back upon you with added power. While thoughts that are calm, pure, and unselfish are so many angelic messengers sent out into the world with health, healing, and blessedness upon their wings, counteracting the evil forces, pouring the oil of joy upon the troubled waters of anxiety and sorrow and restoring to broken hearts their heritage of immortality.

Think good thoughts, and they will quickly become actualized in your outward life in the form of good conditions. Control your soul-forces, and you will be able to shape your outward life as you will. The difference between a savior and a sinner is this: that the one has a perfect control of all the forces within him or her; the other is dominated and controlled by them.

There is absolutely no other way to true power and abiding peace but by self-control, self-government, and self-purification. To be at the mercy of your disposition is to be impotent, unhappy, and of little real use in the world. The conquest of your petty likes and dislikes, your capricious loves and hates, your fits of anger, suspicion, jealousy, and all the changing moods to which you are more or less helplessly subject—this is the task you have before you if you would weave into the web of life the golden threads of happiness and prosperity. Insofar as you are enslaved by the changing moods within you, you will need to depend upon others and upon outward aids as you walk through life.

If you would walk firmly and securely and would accomplish any achievement, you must learn to rise above and control all such disturbing and retarding vibrations. You must daily practice the habit of putting your mind at rest, "going into the silence," as it is commonly called. This is a method of replacing a troubled thought with one of peace, a thought of weakness with one of strength. Until you succeed in doing this, you cannot hope to direct your mental forces upon the problems and pursuits of life with any appreciable measure of success. It is a process of diverting one's scattered forces into one powerful channel. Just as a useless marsh may be converted into a field of golden corn or a fruitful garden by draining and directing the scattered and harmful streams into one well-cut channel, so, by acquiring calmness, and subduing and directing the thought-currents within yourself, you will save your soul and enhance your heart and life.

As you succeed in gaining mastery over your impulses and thoughts, you will begin to feel growing up within you a new and silent power, and a settled feeling of composure and strength will remain with you. Your latent powers will begin to unfold themselves, and whereas formerly your efforts were weak and ineffectual, you will now be able to work with that calm confidence which commands success. And along with this new power and strength, there will be awakened within you that interior illumination known as intuition, and you will walk no longer in darkness and speculation but in light and certainty. With the development of this soul-vision, judgment and mental penetration will be incalculably increased, and there will evolve within you that prophetic vision by the aid of which you will be able to sense coming events and to forecast, with remarkable accuracy, the result of your efforts. And in just the measure that you alter from within will your outlook upon life alter. As you alter your mental attitude toward others, they will alter in their attitude and conduct toward you. As you rise above the lower, debilitating, and destructive thought-forces, you will come in contact with the positive, strengthening, and upbuilding currents generated by strong, pure, and noble minds, your happiness will be immeasurably intensified, and you will begin to realize the joy, strength, and power which are born only of self-mastery. This joy, strength, and power will be continually radiating from you, and without any effort on your part, though you are utterly unconscious of it, strong people will be drawn toward you, influence will be put into your hands, and in accordance with your altered thought-world will outward events shape themselves.

To continue to be strong, useful, and happy, you must cease to be a passive receptacle for the negative, beggarly, and impure streams of thought. You must learn to command your desires and to say, with authority, what thoughts you shall admit into the mansion of your soul. Even a very partial success in self-mastery adds greatly to one's power, and those who succeed in perfecting this divine accomplishment enter into possession of undreamed-of wisdom and inward strength and peace. Such people realize that all the forces of the universe aid and protect their footsteps because they are the masters of their souls.

THE SECRET OF HEALTH, SUCCESS, AND POWER

We all remember with what intense delight, as children, we listened to the never-tiring fairy tale. How eagerly we followed the fluctuating fortunes of the good boy or girl, ever protected, in the hour of crisis, from the evil machinations of the scheming witch, the cruel giant, or the wicked king. And our little hearts never faltered for the fate of the hero or heroine; nor did we doubt their ultimate triumph over all their enemies, for we knew that the fairies were infallible and that they would never desert those who had consecrated themselves to the good and the true. And what unspeakable joy pulsated within us when the Fairy Queen, bringing all her magic to bear at the critical moment, scattered all the darkness and trouble and granted them the complete satisfaction of all their hopes, and they were "happy ever after."

With the accumulating years, and an ever-increasing intimacy with the so-called realities of life, our beautiful fairy world became obliterated, and its wonderful inhabitants were relegated, in the archives of memory, to the shadowy and unreal. And we thought we were wise and strong in thus leaving forever the land of childish dreams, but as we had become little children in the wondrous world of wisdom, we shall return again to the inspiring dreams of childhood and find that they are, after all, realities.

The fairy folk, so small and nearly always invisible yet possessed of an all-conquering and magical power, who bestow upon the good, health, wealth, and happiness along with all the gifts of nature in lavish profusion, start again into reality and become immortalized in the soul-realm of those who, by growth in wisdom, have entered into a knowledge of the power of thought and the laws which govern the inner world of being. To them the fairies live again as thought-people, thought-messengers, and thought-powers working in harmony with the overruling Good. And they who day by day endeavor to harmonize their hearts with the heart of the Supreme Good do in reality acquire true health, wealth, and happiness. There is no protection to compare with goodness, and by "goodness" I do not mean a mere outward conformity to the rules of morality; I mean pure thought, noble aspiration, unselfish love, and freedom from vainglory. To dwell continually in good thoughts is to throw around oneself a psychic atmosphere of sweetness and power that leaves its impress upon all who come in contact with it.

As the rising sun puts to rout the helpless shadows, so are all the impotent forces of evil put to flight by the searching rays of positive thought which shine forth from a heart made strong in purity and faith.

Where there is sterling faith and uncompromising purity, there is health, there is success, there is power. In such a one, disease, failure, and disaster can find no lodgment, for there is nothing on which they can feed.

Even physical conditions are largely determined by mental states, and to this truth the scientific world is rapidly being drawn. The old materialistic belief that we are what our body makes us is rapidly passing away and is being replaced by the inspiring belief that we are superior to our bodies and that our bodies are what we make them by the power of thought. The belief that people are despairing because they are dyspeptic has been replaced with the understanding that they are dyspeptic because they are despairing, and in the near future, the fact that all disease has its origin in the mind will become common knowledge.

There is no evil in the universe but has its root and origin in the mind, and sin, sickness, sorrow, and affliction do not, in reality, belong to the universal order, are not inherent in the nature of things but are the direct outcome of our ignorance of the right relations of things.

According to tradition, there once lived in India a school of philosophers who led a life of such absolute purity and simplicity that they commonly reached the age of one hundred and fifty years, and to fall sick was looked upon by them as an unpardonable disgrace, for it was considered to indicate a violation of law.

The sooner we realize and acknowledge that sickness, far from being the arbitrary visitation of an offended God or the test of an unwise Providence, is the result of our own error or sin, the sooner shall we enter upon the highway of health. Disease comes to those who attract it, to those whose minds and bodies are receptive to it, and flees from those whose strong, pure, and positive thought-sphere generates healing and life-giving currents.

If you are given to anger, worry, jealousy, greed, or

any other inharmonious state of mind and expect perfect physical health, you are expecting the impossible, for you are continually sowing the seeds of disease in your mind. If you would be free from all physical aches and pains and would enjoy perfect physical harmony, then put your mind in order and harmonize your thoughts. Think joyful thoughts; think loving thoughts; let the elixir of goodwill course through your veins, and you will need no other medicine. Put away your jealousies, your suspicions, your worries, your hatreds, your selfish indulgences, and you will put away your dyspepsia, your biliousness, your nervousness and aching joints. If you will persist in clinging to these debilitating and demoralizing habits of mind, then do not complain when your body is laid low with sickness.

The following story illustrates the close relation that exists between habits of mind and bodily conditions: a certain man was afflicted with a painful disease, and he tried one physician after another but all to no purpose. He then visited towns that were famous for their curative waters and, after having bathed in them all, his disease was more painful than ever. One night he dreamed that a Presence came to him and said, "Brother, hast thou tried all the means of cure?" and he replied, "I have tried all." "Nay," said the Presence, "Come with me, and I will show thee a healing bath which has escaped thy notice." The afflicted man followed, and the Presence led him to a clear pool of water, and said, "Plunge thyself in this water and thou shalt surely recover," and thereupon vanished. The man plunged into the water, and on coming out, lo! his disease had left him. At the same moment he saw written above the pool the word "Renounce." Upon waking, the full meaning of his dream flashed across his mind, and looking within he discovered that he had all along been a victim to a sinful indulgence, and he vowed that he would renounce it forever. He carried out his vow and from that day his affliction began to leave him, and in a short time he was completely restored to health.

Many people complain that they have broken down through overwork. In the majority of such cases the breakdown is more frequently the result of foolishly wasted energy. If you would secure health, you must learn to work without friction. To become anxious or excited or to worry over needless details is to invite a breakdown. Work, whether of brain or body, is beneficial and health-giving, and those who can work with a steady and calm persistency, freed from all anxiety and worry and with their minds utterly oblivious to all but the work in hand, will not only accomplish far more than those who are always hurried and anxious, but they will retain their health—a boon which the others quickly forfeit.

True health and true success go together, for they are inseparably intertwined in the thought-realm. As mental harmony produces bodily health, so it also leads to a harmonious sequence in the actual working out of your plans. Order your thoughts and you will order your life. Pour the oil of tranquility upon the turbulent waters of the passions and prejudices, and the tempests of misfortune, howsoever they may threaten, will be powerless to wreck the ship of your soul as it threads its way across the ocean of life. And if that ship be piloted by a cheerful and never-failing faith, its course will be doubly sure and many perils will pass it by which would otherwise attack it.

By the power of faith every enduring work is accomplished. You must have faith in the Supreme, faith in the overruling law, faith in your work and in your power to accomplish that work. This is the rock upon which you must build if you would achieve, if you would stand and not fall. You must follow under all circumstances the highest promptings within you. You must always be true to the divine self, to rely upon the inward light, the inward voice. You must pursue your purpose with a fearless and restful heart, believing that the future will satisfy your every thought and effort. You must believe that the laws of the universe can never fail.

This is faith and the living of faith. By the power of such a faith the dark waters of uncertainty are divided, every mountain of difficulty crumbles away, and the believing soul passes on unharmed. Strive to acquire, above everything, the priceless possession of this dauntless faith, for it is the talisman of happiness, of success, of peace, of power, of all that makes life great and superior to suffering. Build upon such a faith and you build upon the Rock of the Eternal and with the materials of the Eternal, and the structure that you erect will never be dissolved, for it will transcend all the accumulations of material luxuries and riches, the end of which is dust. Whether you are hurled into the depths of sorrow or lifted upon the heights of joy, ever retain your hold upon this faith, ever return to it as your rock of refuge and keep your feet firmly planted upon its immortal and immovable base. Centered in such a faith, you will become possessed of such a spiritual strength as will shatter, like so many toys of glass, all the forces of evil that are hurled against you, and you will achieve a success such as the mere striver after worldly gain can never know or even dream of. There are men and women who have realized this faith, who live in it and by it day by day and who, having put it to the uttermost test, have entered into the possession of its glory and peace. Such have sent out the word of command, and the mountains of sorrow and disappointment, of mental weariness and physical pain, have passed from them and have been cast into the sea of oblivion.

If you will become possessed of this faith, you will not need to trouble about your success or failure, and success will come. You will not need to become anxious about results but will work joyfully and peacefully, knowing that right thoughts and right efforts will inevitably bring about right results.

I know a woman who has entered into many blissful satisfactions, and recently a friend remarked to her, "Oh, how fortunate you are! You only have to wish for a thing, and it comes to you." And it did, indeed, appear so on the surface, but in reality all the blessedness that has entered into this woman's life is the direct outcome of the inward state of blessedness which she has, throughout life, been cultivating and training toward perfection. Mere wishing brings nothing but disappointment; it is living that tells. The foolish wish and grumble; the wise work and wait. And this woman had worked, worked without and within, but especially within upon heart and soul; and with the invisible hands of the spirit she had built up, with the precious stones of faith, hope, joy, devotion, and love, a fair temple of light, whose glorifying radiance was ever round about her. It beamed in her eye; it shone through her countenance; it vibrated in her voice; and all who came into her presence felt its captivating spell.

As it is with her, so it can be with you. Your success, your failure, your influence, your whole life you carry about with you, for your dominant trends of thought are the determining factors in your destiny. Send forth loving, stainless, and happy thoughts, and blessings will fall into your hands and your table will be spread with the cloth of peace. Send forth hateful, impure, and unhappy thoughts, and curses will rain down upon you, and fear and unrest will wait upon your pillow. You are the unconditional maker of your fate, be that fate what it may. Every moment you are sending forth from you the influences that will make or mar your life. Let your heart grow large and loving and unselfish, and great and lasting will be your influence and success, even though you make little money. Confine it within the narrow limits of self-interest, and even though you become a

millionaire, your influence and success at the final reck-
oning will be found to be utterly insignificant.

Cultivate, then, this pure and unselfish spirit and
combine it with purity and faith, singleness of purpose,
and you are evolving from within the elements not only
of abounding health and enduring success but of great-
ness and power.

If your present position is distasteful to you and your
heart is not in your work, nevertheless perform your duties
with scrupulous diligence and, while resting your mind in
the idea that the better position and greater opportunities
are waiting for you, ever keep an active mental outlook for
budding possibilities so that, when the critical moment
arrives and the new channel presents itself, you will step
into it with your mind fully prepared for the undertaking
and with that intelligence and foresight which is born of
mental discipline.

Whatever your task may be, concentrate your whole
mind upon it, throw into it all the energy of which you
are capable. The faultless completion of small tasks leads
inevitably to larger tasks. See to it that you rise by steady
climbing, and you will never fall. And herein lies the
secret of true power. Learn, by constant practice, how to
husband your resources and to concentrate them at any
moment upon a given point. The foolish waste all their

mental and spiritual energy in frivolity, foolish chatter, or selfish argument, not to mention wasteful physical excesses.

If you would acquire overcoming power, you must cultivate poise and passivity. You must be able to stand alone. All power is associated with immovability. The mountain, the massive rock, the storm-tried oak, all speak to us of power because of their combined solitary grandeur and defiant fixity; while the shifting sand, the yielding twig, and the waving reed speak to us of weakness because they are movable and nonresistant and are utterly useless when detached from other people. People of power remain calm and unmoved even when all around them are swayed by some emotion or passion.

You cannot be fit to command and control unless you have succeeded in commanding and controlling yourself. The hysterical, the fearful, the thoughtless and frivolous, let such seek company or they will fall for lack of support; but the calm, the fearless, the thoughtful, and grave, let such seek the solitude of the forest, the desert, and the mountaintop and to their power more power will be added, and they will more and more successfully stem the psychic currents and whirlpools which engulf humankind.

Passion is not power; it is the abuse of power, the dispersion of power. Passion is like a furious storm that beats fiercely and wildly upon the embattled rock, while power is like the rock itself, which remains silent and unmoved through it all. That was a manifestation of true power when Martin Luther, wearied with the persuasions of his fearful friends, who were doubtful as to his safety should he go to Worms, replied, "If there were as many devils in Worms as there are tiles on the housetops I would go." And when Benjamin Disraeli, who would later become Great Britain's prime minister, broke down in his first Parliamentary speech and brought upon himself the derision of the House, that was an exhibition of germinal power when he exclaimed, "The day will come when you will consider it an honor to listen to me."

When that young man, whom I knew, passing through continual reverses and misfortunes, was mocked by his friends and told to desist from further effort, and he replied, "The time is not far distant when you will marvel at my good fortune and success," he showed that he was possessed of that silent and irresistible power which has taken him over innumerable difficulties and crowned his life with success.

If you have not this power, you may acquire it by practice, and the beginning of power is likewise the beginning of wisdom. You must commence by over-coming those purposeless trivialities to which you have hitherto been a willing victim. Boisterous and uncontrolled laughter, slander and idle talk, and joking merely to raise a laugh, all these things must be put on one side as so much waste of valuable energy. Saint Paul never showed his wonderful insight into the hidden laws of human progress to greater advantage than when he warned the Ephesians against "foolish talking and jesting which is not convenient," for to dwell habitually in such practices is to destroy all spiritual power and life. As you succeed in rendering yourself impervious to such mental dissipations, you will begin to understand what true power is, and you will then commence to grapple with the more powerful desires and appetites which hold your soul in bondage and bar the way to power, and your further progress will then be made clear.

Above all be of single aim; have a legitimate and useful purpose, and devote yourself unreservedly to it. Let nothing draw you aside. Be eager to learn but slow to beg. Have a thorough understanding of your work and let it be your own. As you proceed, ever following the inward Guide, the infallible Voice, you will pass on from victory to victory and will rise step by step to higher resting places, and your ever-broadening outlook will gradually reveal to you the essential beauty and purpose of life. Self-purified, health will be yours; faith-protected, success will be yours; self-governed, power will be yours, and all that you do will prosper, for, ceasing to be a disjointed unit self-enslaved, you will be in harmony with the great law, working no longer against, but with, the universal life, the Eternal Good. And what health you gain will remain with you; what success you achieve will be beyond all human computation and will never pass away; and what influence and power you wield will continue to increase throughout the ages, for it will be a part of that unchangeable principle which supports the universe.

This, then, is the secret of health—a pure heart and a well-ordered mind; this is the secret of success—an unfaltering faith and a wisely directed purpose; and to rein in with unfaltering will the dark steed of desire—this is the secret of power.

THE SECRET OF
ABOUNDING HAPPINESS

reat is the thirst for happiness, and equally great is the lack of happiness. The majority of the poor long for riches, believing that their possession would bring them supreme and lasting happiness. Many who are rich, having gratified every desire and whim, suffer from ennui and repletion and are further from the possession of happiness even than the very poor. If we reflect upon this state of things, it will ultimately lead us to a knowledge of the all-important truth that happiness is not derived from mere outward possessions, nor misery from the lack of them; for if this were so, we should find the poor always miserable and the rich always happy, whereas the reverse is frequently the case. Some of the most wretched people whom I have known were those who were surrounded with riches and luxury, while some of the brightest and happiest people I have met were possessed of only the barest necessities of life. Many people who have accumulated riches have confessed that the selfish gratification that followed the acquisition of riches has robbed life of its sweetness and that they were never so happy as when they were poor.

What, then, is happiness and how is it to be secured? Is it a figment, a delusion, and is suffering alone perennial?

We shall find, after earnest observation and reflection, that all, except those who have entered the way of wisdom, believe that happiness is only to be obtained by the gratification of desire. It is this belief, rooted in the soil of ignorance and continually watered by selfish cravings, that is the cause of all the misery in the world. And I do not limit the word "desire" to the grosser animal cravings; it extends to the higher psychic realm, where far more powerful, subtle, and insidious cravings hold in bondage the intellectual and refined, depriving them of all that beauty, harmony, and purity of soul whose expression is happiness.

Most people will admit that selfishness is the cause of all the unhappiness in the world, but they fall under the soul-destroying delusion that it is somebody else's selfishness and not their own. When you are willing to admit that all your unhappiness is the result of your own selfishness, you will not be far from the gates of Paradise; but so long as you are convinced that it is the selfishness of others that is robbing you of joy, so long will you remain a prisoner in your self-created purgatory.

Happiness is that inward state of perfect satisfaction which is joy and peace, and from which all desire is eliminated. The satisfaction that results from gratified desire is brief and illusionary and is always followed by an increased demand for gratification. Desire is as insatiable as the ocean and clamors louder and louder as its demands are attended to. It claims ever-increasing service from its deluded devotees, until at last they are struck down with physical or mental anguish and are hurled into the purifying fires of suffering. Desire is the region of hell, and all torments are centered there. The giving up of desire is the realization of heaven, and all delights await the pilgrim there.

I sent my soul through the invisible,
   Some letter of that afterlife to spell,
   And by-and-by my soul returned to me,
And whispered, "I myself am heaven and hell."

Heaven and hell are inward states. Sink into self and all its gratifications and you sink into hell; rise above self into that state of consciousness that is the utter denial and forgetfulness of self and you enter heaven. Self is blind, without judgment, not possessed of true knowledge, and always leads to suffering. Correct perception, unbiased judgment, and true knowledge belong only to the divine state, and only insofar as you realize this divine consciousness can you know what real happiness is. So long as you persist in selfishly seeking for your own personal happiness, so long will happiness elude you, and you will be sowing the seeds of wretchedness. Insofar as you succeed in losing yourself in the service of others, in that measure will happiness come to you, and you will reap a harvest of bliss.

It is in loving, not in being loved
 The heart is blessed
 It is in giving, not in seeking gifts,
 We find our quest.
 Whatever be thy longing or thy need,
 That do thou give
 So shall thy soul be fed,
and thou indeed shall truly live.

Cling to self and you cling to sorrow; relinquish self and you enter into peace. To seek selfishly is not only to lose happiness but even that which we believe to be the source of happiness. See how gluttons are continually looking about for a new delicacy wherewith to stimulate their deadened appetites, and how, bloated, burdened, and diseased, scarcely any food at last is eaten with pleasure. Whereas those who have mastered their appetites, and not only do not seek but never think of gustatory pleasure, find delight in the most frugal meal. The angel-form of happiness, which we, looking through the eyes of self, imagine we see in gratified desire, when clasped is always found to be the skeleton of misery. Truly, "those that seek their life shall lose it, and those that lose their life shall find it."

Abiding happiness will come to you when, ceasing to selfishly cling, you are willing to give up. When you are willing to lose, unreservedly, that impermanent thing which is so dear to you and which, whether you cling to it or not, will one day be snatched from you, then you will find that that which seemed to you like a painful loss turns out to be a supreme gain. To give up in order to gain—there is no greater delusion than this, nor no more prolific source of misery; but to be willing to yield up and to suffer loss, this is indeed the Way of Life.

How is it possible to find real happiness by centering ourselves in those things that, by their very nature, must pass away? Abiding and real happiness can only be found by centering ourselves in that which is permanent. Rise, therefore, above the clinging to and the craving for impermanent things, and you will then enter into a consciousness of the Eternal, and as, rising above self and by growing more and more into the spirit of purity, self-sacrifice, and universal love, you become centered in that consciousness, you will realize that happiness which has no reaction and which can never be taken from you.

The heart that has reached utter self-forgetfulness in its love for others has not only become possessed of the highest happiness but has entered into immortality, for it has realized the Divine. Look back upon your life and you will find that the moments of your most supreme happiness were those in which you uttered some word, or performed some act, of compassion or self-denying love.

Spiritually, happiness and harmony are synonymous. Harmony is one phase of the great law whose spiritual expression is love. All selfishness is discord, and to be selfish is to be out of harmony with the divine order. As we realize that all-embracing love which is the negation of self, we put ourselves in harmony with the divine music, the universal song, and that ineffable melody which is true happiness becomes our own.

Men and women are rushing hither and thither in the blind search for happiness and cannot find it; nor ever will, until they recognize that happiness is already within them and round about them, filling the universe, and that they in their selfish searching are shutting themselves out from it.

I followed happiness to make her mine,
    Past towering oak and swinging ivy vine.
    She fled, I chased, o'er slanting hill and dale,
    O'er fields and meadows, in the purpling vale.
    Pursuing rapidly o'er dashing stream,
    I scaled the dizzy cliffs where the eagles scream;
    I traversed swiftly every land and sea,
    But always happiness eluded me.
    Exhausted, fainting, I pursued no more,
    But sank to rest upon a barren shore.
    One came and asked for food, and one for alms;
    I placed the bread and gold in bony palms;
    One came for sympathy, and one for rest;
    I shared with every needy one my best;
    When lo! sweet Happiness, with form divine,
Stood by me, whispering softly, "I am thine."

These beautiful lines of Burleigh's express the secret of all abounding happiness. Sacrifice the personal and transient, and you rise at once into the impersonal and permanent. Give up that narrow cramped self that seeks to render all things subservient to its own petty interests, and you will enter into the company of the angels, into the very heart and essence of universal love. Forget yourself entirely in the sorrows of others and in ministering to others, and divine happiness will emancipate you from all sorrow and suffering.

"Taking the first step with a good thought, the second with a good word, and the third with a good deed, I entered Paradise." And you also may enter into Paradise by pursuing the same course. It is not beyond; it is here. It is realized only by the unselfish. It is known in its fullness only to the pure in heart.

If you have not realized this unbounded happiness, you may begin to actualize it by ever holding before you the lofty ideal of unselfish love and aspiring toward it. Aspiration or prayer is desire turned upward. It is the soul turning toward its divine source, where alone permanent satisfaction can be found. By aspiration the destructive forces of desire are transmuted into divine and all-preserving energy. To aspire is to make an effort to shake off the trammels of desire; it is the prodigal son, made wise by loneliness and suffering, returning to his Father's Mansion.

As you rise above the sordid self; as you break, one after another, the chains that bind you, will you realize the joy of giving, as distinguished from the misery of grasping giving of your substance; giving of your intellect; giving of the love and light that is growing within you. You will then understand that it is indeed "more blessed to give than to receive." But the giving must be of the heart without any taint of self, without desire for reward. The gift of pure love is always attended with bliss. If, after you have given, you are wounded because you are not thanked or flattered or your name put in the paper, know then that your gift was prompted by vanity and not by love, and you were merely giving in order to get, were not really giving but grasping.

Lose yourself in the welfare of others; forget yourself in all that you do; this is the secret of abounding happiness. Ever be on the watch to guard against selfishness, and learn faithfully the divine lessons of inward sacrifice; so shall you climb the highest heights of happiness and shall remain in the never-clouded sunshine of universal joy, clothed in the shining garment of immortality.

THE REALIZATION OF
PROSPERITY

I t is granted only to the heart that abounds with integrity, trust, generosity, and love to realize true prosperity. The heart that is not possessed of these qualities cannot know prosperity, for prosperity, like happiness, is not an outward possession but an inward realization. Greedy people may become millionaires, but they will always be wretched, and mean, and poor, and will even consider themselves outwardly poor so long as there is another person in the world who is richer than they are, while the upright, the open-handed, and the loving will realize a full and rich prosperity, even though their outward possessions may be small.

When we contemplate the fact that the universe is abounding in all good things, material as well as spiritual, and compare it to the blind eagerness to secure a few gold coins or a few acres of dirt, it is then that we realize how dark and ignorant selfishness is. It is then that we know that self-seeking is self-destruction.

Nature gives all, without reservation, and loses nothing; those grasping all lose everything. If you would realize true prosperity do not settle down, as many have done, into the belief that if you do right, everything will go wrong. Do not allow the word "competition" to shake your faith in the supremacy of righteousness. I do not care what people may say about the "laws of competition," for I know the unchangeable law, which shall one day put them all to rout and which puts them to rout even now in the heart and life of the righteous— and knowing this law, I can contemplate all dishonesty with undisturbed repose, for I know where certain destruction awaits it.

Under all circumstances, do that which you believe to be right, and trust the law; trust the Divine Power that is imminent in the universe, and it will never desert you, and you will always be protected. By such a trust all your losses will be converted into gains, and all curses that threaten will be transmuted into blessings. Never let go of integrity, generosity, and love, for these, coupled with energy, will lift you into the truly prosperous state. Do not believe the world when it tells you that you must always attend to "number one" first, and to others afterward. To do this is not to think of others at all but only of one's own comforts. To those who practice this, the day will come when all will desert them, and when they cry out in their loneliness and anguish, there will be no one to hear and help them. To consider one's self before all others is to cramp and warp and hinder every noble and divine impulse. Let your soul expand, let your heart reach out to others in loving and generous warmth, and great and lasting will be your joy and all prosperity will come to you.

Those who have wandered from the highway of righteousness guard themselves against competition. Those who always pursue the right do not have to trouble about such defense. This is no empty statement. There are people today who, by the power of integrity and faith, have defied all competition, and who, without swerving in the least from their methods, when competed with, have risen steadily into prosperity, while those who tried to undermine them have fallen back defeated.

To possess those inward qualities which constitute

goodness is to be armored against all the powers of evil and to be doubly protected in every time of trial; and to build oneself up in those qualities is to build up a success which cannot be shaken and to enter into a prosperity which will endure forever.

PART 2

The WAY
of PEACE

THE POWER OF
MEDITATION

S piritual meditation is the pathway to Divinity. It is the mystic ladder that reaches from earth to heaven, from error to truth, from pain to peace. Every saint has climbed it; every sinner must sooner or later come to it, and all weary pilgrims who turn their backs upon self and the world and set their faces resolutely toward the Father's Home must plant their feet upon its golden rounds. Without its aid, you cannot grow into the divine state, the divine likeness, the divine peace, and the fadeless glories and nonpolluting joys of truth will remain hidden from you.

Meditation is the intense dwelling, in thought, upon an idea or theme, with the object of thoroughly comprehending it, and whatsoever you constantly meditate upon, you not only will come to understand but will grow more and more into its likeness, for it will become incorporated into your very being, will become, in fact, your very self. If, therefore, you constantly dwell upon that which is selfish and debasing, you will ultimately become selfish and debased; if you ceaselessly think upon that which is pure and unselfish, you will surely become pure and unselfish.

Tell me what that is upon which you most frequently and intensely think, that to which, in your silent hours, your soul most naturally turns, and I will tell you to what place of pain or peace you are traveling and whether you are growing into the likeness of the divine or the bestial.

There is an unavoidable tendency to become literally the embodiment of that quality upon which one most constantly thinks. Let, therefore, the object of your meditation be above and not below, so that every time you revert to it in thought you will be lifted up; let it be pure and unmixed with any selfish element; so shall your heart become purified and drawn nearer to truth and not be defiled and dragged more hopelessly into error.

Meditation, in the spiritual sense in which I am now using it, is the secret of all growth in spiritual life and knowledge. Every prophet, sage, and savior became such by the power of meditation. Buddha meditated upon the truth until he could say, "I am the Truth." Jesus brooded upon the divine imminence until at last he could declare, "I and my Father are One."

Meditation centered upon divine realities is the very essence and soul of prayer. It is the silent reaching of the soul toward the Eternal. Mere petitionary prayer without meditation is a body without a soul and is powerless to lift the mind and heart above sin and affliction. If you are daily praying for wisdom, for peace, for loftier purity and a fuller realization of truth, and that for which you pray is still far from you, it means that you are praying for one thing while living out in thought and act another. If you will cease from such waywardness, taking your mind off those things the selfish clinging to which debars you from the possession of the stainless realities for which you pray; if you will no longer ask God to grant you that which you do not deserve, or to bestow upon you that love and compassion which you refuse to bestow upon others, but will commence to think and act in the spirit of truth, you will day by day be growing into those realities, so that ultimately you will become one with them.

If you would secure any worldly advantage, you must be willing to work vigorously for it and would be foolish indeed to wait with folded hands, expecting it to come to you for the mere asking. Do not then vainly imagine that you can obtain the heavenly possessions without making an effort. Only when you commence to work earnestly in the kingdom of truth will you be allowed to partake of the bread of life, and when you have, by patient and uncomplaining effort, earned the spiritual wages for which you ask, they will not be withheld from you.

If you really seek truth, and not merely your own gratification; if you love it above all worldly pleasures and gains, more even than happiness itself, you will be willing to make the effort necessary for its achievement.

If you would be freed from sin and sorrow; if you would taste of that spotless purity for which you sigh and pray; if you would realize wisdom and knowledge and would enter into the possession of profound and abiding peace, come now and enter the path of meditation, and let the supreme object of your meditation be truth.

At the outset, meditation must be distinguished from idle reverie. There is nothing dreamy and unpractical about it. It is a process of searching and uncompromising thought that allows nothing to remain but the simple and naked truth. Meditating in this way, you will no longer strive to build yourself up in your prejudices, but forgetting self, you will remember only that you are seeking the truth. And so you will remove, one by one, the errors that you have built around yourself in the past and will patiently wait for the revelation of truth that will come when your errors have been sufficiently removed. In the silent humility of your heart you will realize that

> There is an inmost center in us all
>> Where truth abides in fullness; and around,
>> Wall upon wall, the gross flesh hems it in;
>> This perfect, clear perception, which is Truth,
>> A baffling and perverted carnal mesh
>> Binds it, and makes all error; and to know,
>> Rather consists in opening out a way
>> Whence the imprisoned splendor may escape,
>> Than in effecting entry for a light
> Supposed to be without.

Select some portion of the day in which to meditate and keep that period sacred to your purpose. The best time is the very early morning when the spirit of repose is upon everything. All natural conditions will then be in your favor: the passions, after the long bodily fast of the night, will be subdued; the excitements and worries of the previous day will have died away; and the mind, strong and yet restful, will be receptive to spiritual instruction. Indeed, one of the first efforts you will be called upon to make will be to shake off lethargy and indulgence, and if you refuse, you will be unable to advance, for the demands of the spirit are imperative.

To be spiritually awakened is also to be mentally and physically awakened. The sluggard and the self-indulgent can have no knowledge of truth. If those who are possessed of health and strength waste the calm, precious hours of the silent morning in drowsy indulgence, they are totally unfit to climb the heavenly heights.

Those whose awakening consciousness have become alive to its lofty possibilities, who are beginning to shake off the darkness of ignorance in which the world is enveloped, rise before the stars have ceased their vigil, and grappling with the darkness within their souls, strive by holy aspiration to perceive the light of truth while the unawakened world dreams on.

The heights by great men reached and kept,
  Were not attained by sudden flight,
  But they, while their companions slept,
Were toiling upward in the night.

No saint, no holy man, no teacher of truth, ever lived who did not rise early in the morning. Jesus habitually rose early and climbed the solitary mountains to engage in holy communion. Buddha always rose an hour before sunrise and engaged in meditation, and all his disciples were enjoined to do the same.

If you have to commence your daily duties at a very early hour and are thus debarred from giving the early morning to systematic meditation, try to give an hour at night, and should this, by the length and laboriousness of your daily task be denied you, you need not despair, for you may turn your thoughts upward in holy meditation in the intervals of your work or in those few idle minutes which you now waste in aimlessness. Should your work be of that kind that becomes by practice automatic, you may meditate while engaged upon it. That eminent philosopher Jakob Böhme realized his vast knowledge of divine things while working long hours as a shoemaker. In every life there is time to think, and the busiest, the most laborious, is not shut out from aspiration and meditation.

Spiritual meditation and self-discipline are inseparable; you will therefore commence to meditate upon yourself so as to try and understand yourself, for, remember, the great object you will have in view will be the complete removal of all your errors in order that you may realize truth. You will begin to question your motives, thoughts, and acts, comparing them to your ideal and endeavoring to look upon them with a calm and impartial eye. In this manner you will continually be gaining more of that mental and spiritual equilibrium without which men are but helpless straws upon the ocean of life. If you are given to hatred or anger, you will meditate upon gentleness and forgiveness, so as to become actually alive to a sense of your harsh and foolish conduct. You will then begin to dwell in thoughts of love, of gentleness, of abounding forgiveness; and as you overcome the lower by the higher, there will gradually, silently steal into your heart a knowledge of the divine law of love with an understanding of its bearing upon all the intricacies of life and conduct. In applying this knowledge to your every thought, word, and act, you will grow more and more gentle, more and more loving, more and more divine. And thus with every error, every selfish desire, every human weakness: by the power of meditation is it overcome, and as each sin, each error, is thrust out, a fuller and clearer measure of the light of truth illumines the pilgrim soul.

By meditating, you will be ceaselessly fortifying yourself against your only real enemy, your selfish, perishable self, and will be establishing yourself more and more firmly in the divine and imperishable self that is inseparable from truth. The direct outcome of your meditations will be a calm, spiritual strength that will be your stay and resting place in the struggle of life. Great is the overcoming power of holy thought, and the strength and knowledge gained in the hour of silent meditation will enrich the soul with saving remembrance in the hour of strife, of sorrow, or of temptation.

As, by the power of meditation, you grow in wisdom, you will relinquish, more and more, your selfish desires which are fickle, impermanent, and productive of sorrow and pain, and will take your stand, with increasing steadfastness and trust, upon unchangeable principles and will realize heavenly rest.

The use of meditation is the acquisition of a knowledge of eternal principles, and the power which results from meditation is the ability to rest upon and trust those principles, and so become one with the Eternal. The end of meditation is, therefore, direct knowledge of truth, God, and the realization of divine and profound peace.

Let your meditations take their rise from the ethical ground that you now occupy. Remember that you are to grow into truth by steady perseverance. Do not be as those who consider themselves "religious" but who fail to meditate upon the law of truth, who practice only those precepts that are specific to their particular creeds, and who continue in the ceaseless round of sin and suffering. Strive to rise, by the power of meditation, above all selfish clinging to partial gods or party creeds above dead formalities and lifeless ignorance. Thus walking the highway of wisdom, with mind fixed upon the spotless truth, you shall know no halting place short of the realization of truth. Those who earnestly meditate first perceive a truth, as it were, afar off and then realize it by daily practice. It is only the doer of the word of truth that can know of the doctrine of truth, for though by pure thought the truth is perceived, it is actualized only by practice.

Said the divine Gautama, the Buddha, "He who gives himself up to vanity, and does not give himself up to meditation, forgetting the real aim of life and grasping at pleasure, will in time envy him who has exerted himself in meditation." He instructed his disciples in the following Five Great Meditations:

The first meditation is the meditation of love, in which you so adjust your heart that you long for the welfare of all beings, including the happiness of your enemies.

The second meditation is the meditation of pity, in which you think of all beings in distress, vividly representing in your imagination their sorrows and anxieties so as to arouse a deep compassion for them in your soul.

The third meditation is the meditation of joy, in which you think of the prosperity of others and rejoice with their rejoicings.

The fourth meditation is the meditation of impurity, in which you consider the evil consequences of corruption, the effects of sin and diseases. How trivial often the pleasure of the moment and how fatal its consequences.

The fifth meditation is the meditation on serenity, in which you rise above love and hate, tyranny and oppression, wealth and want, and regard your own fate with impartial calmness and perfect tranquility.

By engaging in these meditations, the disciples of the Buddha arrived at knowledge of the truth. But whether you engage in these particular meditations or not matters little so long as your object is truth, so long as you hunger and thirst for that righteousness which is a holy heart and a blameless life. In your meditations, therefore, let your heart grow and expand with ever-broadening love, until, free from all hatred, and passion, and condemnation, it embraces the whole universe with thoughtful tenderness. As the flower opens its petals to receive the morning light, so too open your soul more and more to the glorious light of truth. Soar upward upon the wings of aspiration; be fearless and believe in the loftiest possibilities. Believe that a life of absolute meekness is possible; believe that a life of stainless purity is possible; believe that a life of perfect holiness is possible; believe that the realization of the highest truth is possible. Those who so believe climb rapidly the heavenly hills, while the unbelievers continue to grope darkly and painfully in the fog-bound valleys.

By so believing, so aspiring, so meditating, divinely sweet and beautiful your spiritual experiences will be. The revelations that enrapture your inward vision will be glorious. As you realize the divine love, the divine justice, the divine purity, the perfect law of good, or God, great will be your bliss and deep your peace. Old things will pass away, and all things will become new. The veil of the material universe, so dense and impenetrable to the eye of error, so thin and gauzy to the eye of truth, will be lifted and the spiritual universe will be revealed. Time will cease, and you will live only in eternity. Change and mortality will no more cause you anxiety and sorrow, for you will become established in the unchangeable and will dwell in the very heart of immortality.

THE TWO MASTERS,
SELF AND TRUTH

Upon the battlefield of the human soul two masters are ever contending for the crown of supremacy, for the kingship and dominion of the heart; the master of self, called also the Prince of this world, and the master of truth, called also the Father God. The master self is that rebellious one whose weapons are passion, pride, avarice, vanity, self-will, implements of darkness; the master truth is that meek and lowly one whose weapons are gentleness, patience, purity, sacrifice, humility, love, instruments of light.

In every soul the battle is waged, and as a soldier cannot engage at once in two opposing armies, so every heart is enlisted either in the ranks of self or of truth. There is no half-and-half course: "There is self and there is truth; where self is, truth is not, where truth is, self is not." Thus spoke Buddha, the teacher of truth, and Jesus declared, "No man can serve two masters; for either he will hate the one and love the other; or else he will hold to the one and despise the other. Ye cannot serve God and Mammon."

Truth is so simple, so absolutely undeviating and uncompromising that it admits of no complexity, no turning, and no qualification. Self is ingenious, crooked, and, governed by subtle and snaky desire, admits of endless turnings and qualifications, and the deluded worshippers of self vainly imagine that they can gratify every worldly desire and at the same time possess the truth. But the lovers of truth worship truth with the sacrifice of self and ceaselessly guard themselves against worldliness and self-seeking.

Do you seek to know and to realize truth? Then you must be prepared to sacrifice, to renounce to the uttermost, for truth in all its glory can be perceived and known only when the last vestige of self has disappeared.

Jesus declared that he who would be His disciple must deny himself daily. Are you willing to deny yourself, to give up your lusts, your prejudices, and your opinions? If so, you may enter the narrow way of truth and find that peace from which the world is shut out.

The absolute denial, the utter extinction, of self is the perfect state of truth, and all religions and philosophies are but so many aids to this supreme attainment.

Self is the denial of truth. Truth is the denial of self. As you let self die, you will be reborn in truth. As you cling to self, truth will be hidden from you. While you cling to self, your path will be beset with difficulties, and repeated pains, sorrows, and disappointments will be your lot. There are no difficulties in truth, and coming to truth, you will be freed from all sorrow and disappointment.

Truth in itself is not hidden and dark. It is always revealed and is perfectly transparent. But the blind and wayward self cannot perceive it. The light of day is not hidden except to the blind, and the light of truth is not hidden except to those who are blinded by self.

Truth is the one reality in the universe, the inward harmony, the perfect justice, the eternal love. Nothing can be added to it or taken from it. It does not depend upon any one person, but all people depend upon it. You cannot perceive the beauty of truth while you are looking out through the eyes of self. If you are vain, you will color everything with your own vanities. If lustful, your heart and mind will be so clouded with the smoke and flames of passion that everything will appear distorted through them. If proud and opinionated, you will see nothing in the whole universe except the magnitude and importance of your own opinions.

There is one quality which preeminently distinguishes people of truth from the people of self, and that is humility. Not only to be free from vanity, stubbornness, and egotism but to regard one's own opinions as of no value, this indeed is true humility.

Those who are immersed in self regard their own opinions as truth, and the opinions of others as error. But humble truth-lovers, who have learned to distinguish between opinion and truth, regard all people with the eye of charity and do not seek to defend their opinions but sacrifice those opinions that they may love the more, that they may manifest the spirit of truth, for truth in its very nature is ineffable and can only be lived. Those who have most of charity have most of truth.

People engage in heated controversies and foolishly imagine they are defending the truth, when in reality they are merely defending their own petty interests and perishable opinions. Followers of self take up arms against others. Followers of truth take up arms against themselves. Truth, being unchangeable and eternal, is independent of your opinion and of mine. We may enter into it or we may stay outside; but both our defense and our attack are superfluous and are hurled back upon ourselves.

Those enslaved by self, passionate, proud, and con-demnatory, believe their particular creed or religion to be the truth and all other religions to be error; and they pros-elytize with passionate ardor. There is but one religion, the religion of truth. There is but one error, the error of self. Truth is not a formal belief; it is an unselfish, holy, and aspiring heart; those who have truth are at peace with all and cherish all with thoughts of love.

You may easily know whether you are a child of truth or a worshipper of self, if you will silently examine your mind, heart, and conduct. Do you harbor thoughts of suspicion, enmity, envy, lust, pride, or do you strenu-ously fight against these? If the former, you are chained to self, no matter what religion you may profess; if the latter, you are a candidate for truth, even though out-wardly you may profess no religion. Are you passionate, self-willed, ever seeking to gain your own ends, self-indulgent, and self-centered; or are you gentle, mild, unselfish, quit of every form of self-indulgence and ever ready to give up your own? If the former, self is your master; if the latter, truth is the object of your affection. Do you strive for riches? Do you fight with passion for your party? Do you lust for power and leadership? Are you given to ostentation and self-praise? Or have you given up the love of riches? Have you relinquished all strife? Are you content to take the lowest place and to be passed by unnoticed? And have you ceased to talk about yourself and to regard yourself with self-complacent pride? If the former, even though you may imagine you worship God, the god of your heart is self. If the latter, even though you may withhold your lips from worship, you are dwelling with the Most High.

The signs by which the truth-lover is known are unmistakable. Hear the holy Krishna declare them, in Sir Edwin Arnold's beautiful rendering of the *Bhavagad Gita*:

> Fearlessness, singleness of soul, the will
>   Always to strive for wisdom; opened hand
>   And governed appetites; and piety
>   And love of lonely study; humbleness,
>   Uprightness, heed to injure nought which lives,
>   Truthfulness, slowness unto wrath, a mind
>   That lightly letteth go what others prize;
>   And equanimity, and charity
>   Which spieth no man's faults; and tenderness
>   Towards all that suffer; a contented heart,
>   Fluttered by no desires; a bearing mild,
>   Modest, and grave, with manhood nobly mixed
>   With patience, fortitude, and purity;

An unrevengeful spirit, never given
To rate itself too high;—such be the signs,
O Indian Prince! of him whose feet are set
On that fair path which leads to heavenly birth!

When those, lost in the devious ways of error and self, have forgotten the "heavenly birth," the state of holiness and truth, they set up artificial standards by which to judge one another and make acceptance of, and adherence to, their own particular theology the test of truth; and so such people are divided one against another, and there is ceaseless enmity and strife and unending sorrow and suffering.

Do you seek to realize the birth into truth? There is only one way: let self die. All those lusts, appetites, desires, opinions, limited conceptions, and prejudices to which you have hitherto so tenaciously clung, let them fall from you. Let them no longer hold you in bondage, and truth will be yours. Cease to look upon your own religion as superior to all others, and strive humbly to learn the supreme lesson of charity. No longer cling to the idea, so productive of strife and sorrow, that the Savior whom you worship is the only Savior, and that the Savior whom your brother worships with equal sincerity and ardor, is an impostor; but seek diligently the path of holiness, and then you will realize that every holy person is a savior of humankind.

The giving up of self is not merely the renunciation of outward things. It consists of the renunciation of the inward sin, the inward error. Not by giving up vain clothing; not by relinquishing riches; not by abstaining from certain foods; not by speaking smooth words; not by merely doing these things is the truth found; but by giving up the spirit of vanity; by relinquishing the desire for riches; by abstaining from the lust of self-indulgence; by giving up all hatred, strife, condemnation, and self-seeking, and becoming gentle and pure at heart; by doing these things is the truth found. To do the former and not to do the latter is hypocrisy, whereas the latter includes the former. You may renounce the outward world and isolate yourself in a cave or in the depths of a forest, but you will take all your selfishness with you, and unless you renounce that, great indeed will be your wretchedness and deep your delusion. You may remain just where you are, performing all your duties, and yet renounce the world, the inward enemy. To be in the world and yet not of the world is the highest perfection, the most blessed peace, is to achieve the greatest victory. The renunciation of self is the way of truth.

Enter the Path; there is no grief like hate,
　　No pain like passion, no deceit like sense
　　Enter the Path; far hath he gone whose foot
Treads down one fond offense.

As you succeed in overcoming self, you will begin to
see things in their right relations. Those who are swayed
by any passions, prejudice, like or dislike, adjust everything to that particular bias and see only their own delusions. Those who are absolutely free from all passion,
prejudice, preference, and partiality see themselves as
they are; see others as they are; see all things in their
proper proportions and right relations. Having nothing
to attack, nothing to defend, nothing to conceal, and no
interests to guard, they are at peace. They have realized
the profound simplicity of truth, for this unbiased, tranquil, blessed state of mind and heart is the state of truth.
Those who attain to it dwell with the angels and sit at
the footstool of the Supreme. Knowing the great law;
knowing the origin of sorrow; knowing the secret of suffering; knowing the way of emancipation in truth, how
can such people engage in strife or condemnation; for
they know that the blind, self-seeking world, surrounded
with the clouds of its own illusions and enveloped in the
darkness of error and self, cannot perceive the steadfast

light of truth and is utterly incapable of comprehending the profound simplicity of the heart that has died, or is dying, to self. Yet they also know that when the suffering ages have piled up mountains of sorrow, the crushed and burdened soul of the world will fly to its final refuge, and that when the ages are completed, every prodigal will come back to the fold of truth. And so they dwell in good will toward all and regard all with that tender compassion which a father bestows upon his wayward children.

People cannot understand truth because they cling to self, because they believe in and love self, because they believe self to be the only reality, whereas it is the one delusion. When you cease to believe in and love self, you will desert it and will fly to truth and will find the eternal reality.

When people are intoxicated with the wines of luxury, and pleasure, and vanity, the thirst of life grows and deepens within them, and they delude themselves with dreams of fleshly immortality, but when they come to reap the harvest of their own sowing, and pain and sorrow supervene, then, crushed and humiliated, relinquishing self and all the intoxications of self, they come, with aching hearts to the one immortality, the immortality that destroys all delusions, the spiritual immortality in truth.

People pass from evil to good, from self to truth, through the dark gate of sorrow, for sorrow and self are inseparable. Only in the peace and bliss of truth is all sorrow vanquished. If you suffer disappointment because your cherished plans have been thwarted or because someone has not come up to your anticipations, it is because you are clinging to self. If you suffer remorse for your conduct, it is because you have given way to self. If you are overwhelmed with chagrin and regret because of the attitude of someone else toward you, it is because you have been cherishing self. If you are wounded on account of what has been done to you or said of you, it is because you are walking in the painful way of self. All suffering is of self. All suffering ends in truth. When you have entered into and realized truth, you will no longer suffer disappointment, remorse, and regret, and sorrow will flee from you.

Self is the only prison that can ever bind the soul;
Truth is the only angel that can bid the gates unroll;
And when he comes to call thee, arise and follow fast;
His way may lie through darkness, but it leads to light at last.

The woe of the world is of its own making. Sorrow purifies and deepens the soul, and the extremity of sorrow is the prelude to truth. Have you suffered much? Have you sorrowed deeply? Have you pondered seriously upon the problem of life? If so, you are prepared to wage war against self and to become a disciple of truth.

The intellectuals who do not see the necessity for giving up self frame endless theories about the universe and call them truth; but if they pursue that direct line of conduct which is the practice of righteousness, they will realize the truth which has no place in theory and which never changes. Cultivate your heart. Water it continually with unselfish love and deep-felt pity, and strive to shut out from it all thoughts and feelings that are not in accordance with love. Return good for evil, love for hatred, gentleness for ill-treatment, and remain silent when attacked. So shall you transmute all your selfish desires into the pure gold of love, and self will disappear in truth. So you will walk blamelessly, yoked with the easy yoke of lowliness and clothed with the divine garment of humility.

THE ACQUISITION OF
SPIRITUAL POWER

The world is filled with men and women seeking pleasure, excitement, novelty; seeking ever to be moved to laughter or tears; not seeking strength, stability, and power; but courting weakness, and eagerly engaged in dispersing what power they have.

Men and women of real power and influence are few because few are prepared to make the sacrifice necessary to the acquisition of power, and fewer still are ready to patiently build up character.

To be swayed by your fluctuating thoughts and impulses is to be weak and powerless; to rightly control and direct those forces is to be strong and powerful. People of strong animal passions have much of the ferocity of the beast, but this is not power. The elements of power are there; but it is only when this ferocity is tamed and subdued by the higher intelligence that real power begins; and people can only grow in power by awakening themselves to higher and ever higher states of intelligence and consciousness.

The difference between people of weakness and people of power lies not in the strength of the personal will (for stubborn people are usually weak and foolish) but in that focus of consciousness which represents their states of knowledge.

The pleasure-seekers, the lovers of excitement, the hunters after novelty, and the victims of impulse and hysterical emotion lack that knowledge of principles which gives balance, stability, and influence.

People commence to develop power when, checking their impulses and selfish inclinations, they fall back upon the higher and calmer consciousness within them and begin to steady themselves upon a principle.

The realization of unchanging principles in consciousness is at once the source and secret of the highest power. When, after much searching, and suffering, and sacrificing, the light of an eternal principle dawns upon the soul, a divine calm ensues and joy unspeakable gladdens the heart.

Those who have realized such a principle cease to

wander and remain poised and self-possessed. They cease to be "passion's slaves" and become master-builders in the Temple of Destiny.

People governed by self and not by a principle change their front when their selfish comforts are threatened. Deeply intent upon defending and guarding their own interests, they regard all means as lawful that will serve that end. They are continually scheming as to how to protect themselves against enemies, being too self-centered to perceive that they are their own enemies. Such people's work crumbles away, for it is divorced from truth and power. All effort that is grounded upon self perishes; only that work endures that is built upon an indestructible principle.

Those who stand upon a principle remain calm, dauntless, and self-possessed under all circumstances. When the hour of trial comes and decision must be made between personal comforts and truth, comforts are given up. This cannot be altered even when they are faced with the prospect of torture.

Self-centered people regard the loss of their wealth, their comforts, or their lives as the greatest calamities which can befall them. People of principle look upon these incidents as comparatively insignificant and not to be compared with loss of character and loss of truth. To desert truth is, to such people, the only happening which can really be called a calamity.

It is the hour of crisis which decides who are the minions of darkness and who the children of light. It is the epoch of threatening disaster, ruin, and persecution which divides the sheep from the goats and reveals to the reverential gaze of succeeding ages the men and women of power.

It is easy for people, so long as they are left in the enjoyment of their possessions, to persuade themselves that they believe in and adhere to the principles of peace, harmony, and universal love; but when their enjoyments are threatened or they imagine they are threatened, they begin to clamor loudly for war. Such people show that they believe in and stand upon, not peace, harmony, and love, but strife, selfishness, and hatred.

Those who do not desert their principles when threatened with the loss of every earthly thing, even to the loss of reputation and life, are the people of power. They are the men and women whose every word and work endures. They represent the leaders whom the afterworld honors, reveres, and worships. There is no way to the acquisition of spiritual power except by that inward illumination and enlightenment which is the realization of spiritual principles; and those principles can be realized only by constant practice and application.

Take the principle of divine love, and quietly and diligently meditate upon it with the object of arriving at a thorough understanding of it. Bring its searching light to bear upon all your habits, your actions, your speech and intercourse with others, your every secret thought and desire. As you persevere in this course, the divine love will become more and more perfectly revealed to you, and your own shortcomings will stand out in more vivid contrast, spurring you on to renewed endeavor. Having once caught a glimpse of the incomparable majesty of that imperishable principle, you will never again rest in your weakness, your selfishness, your imperfection, but will pursue that love until you have relinquished every discordant element and have brought yourself into perfect harmony with it. And that state of inward harmony is spiritual power. Take also other spiritual principles, such as purity and compassion, and apply them in the same way. So exacting is truth, you will be able to make no stay, no resting place until the inmost garment of your soul is bereft of every stain and your heart has become incapable of any hard, condemnatory, and pitiless impulse.

Only insofar as you understand, realize, and rely upon these principles will you acquire spiritual power, and that power will be manifested in and through you in the form of increasing dispassion, patience, and equanimity.

Dispassion argues superior self-control; sublime patience is the very hallmark of divine knowledge, and to retain an unbroken calm amid all the duties and distractions of life marks off the people of power. It is easy in the world to live after the world's opinion; it is easy in solitude to live after our own; but truly great people are those who in the midst of the crowd keep with perfect sweetness the independence of solitude.

Some mystics hold that perfection in dispassion is the source of that power by which miracles (so-called) are performed, and truly those who have gained such perfect control of all their interior forces that no shock, however great, can for one moment unbalance them must be capable of guiding and directing those forces in a consummate manner.

To grow in self-control, in patience, in equanimity, is to grow in strength and power; and you can only thus grow by focusing your consciousness upon a principle. As a child, after making many and vigorous attempts to walk unaided, at last succeeds, after numerous falls, in accomplishing this, so you must enter the way of power by first attempting to stand alone. Break away from the tyranny of custom, tradition, conventionality, and the opinions of others, until you succeed in walking lonely and erect. Rely upon your own judgment; be true to your own conscience; follow the light that is within you; all outward lights are so many will-o'-the wisps. There will be those who will tell you that you are foolish, that your judgment is faulty, that your conscience is all awry, and that the light within you is darkness, but heed them not. If what they say is true, the sooner you as a searcher for wisdom find it out, the better, and you can make the discovery only by bringing your powers to the test. Therefore, pursue your course bravely. Your conscience is at least your own, and to follow it is the path to freedom; to follow the conscience of another is to be condemned to slavery. You will have many falls, will suffer many wounds, will endure many buffetings for a time, but press on in faith, believing that sure and certain victory lies ahead. Search for a rock, a principle, and having found it cling to it; get it under your feet and stand erect upon it until at last, immovably fixed upon it, you succeed in defying the fury of the waves and storms of selfishness. For selfishness in any and every form is dissipation, weakness, death; unselfishness in its spiritual aspect is conservation, power, and life. As you grow in spiritual life and become established upon principles, you will become as beautiful and as unchangeable as those principles, will taste of the sweetness of their immortal essence, and will realize the eternal and indestructible nature of the God within.

THE REALIZATION OF
SELFLESS LOVE

It is said that Michaelangelo saw in every rough block of stone a thing of beauty awaiting the master-hand to bring it into reality. Even so, within each there reposes the divine image awaiting the master-hand of faith and the chisel of patience to bring it into manifestation. And that divine image is revealed and realized as stainless, selfless love.

Hidden deep in every human heart, though frequently covered up with a mass of hard and almost impenetrable accretions, is the spirit of divine love, whose holy and spotless essence is undying and eternal. It is truth; it is that which belongs to the Supreme: that which is real and immortal. All else changes and passes away; this alone is permanent and imperishable; and to realize this love by ceaseless diligence in the practice of the highest righteousness, to live in it and to become fully conscious in it, is to enter into immortality here and now, is to become one with truth, one with God, one with the central heart of all things, and to know our own divine and eternal nature.

To reach this love, to understand and experience it, you must work with great persistency and diligence upon your heart and mind, must ever renew your patience and keep strong your faith, for there will be much to remove, much to accomplish before the divine image is revealed in all its glorious beauty.

Those who strive to reach and to accomplish the divine will be tried to the very uttermost; and this is absolutely necessary, for how else could they acquire that sublime patience without which there is no real wisdom, no divinity? All their work will seem to be futile and their efforts appear to be thrown away. Now and then a hasty touch will mar their image, and perhaps when they imagine their work is almost completed, they will find what they imagined to be the beautiful form of divine love utterly destroyed, and they must begin again with this past bitter experience to guide and help them. But those who have resolutely set themselves to realize the Highest recognize no such thing as defeat. All failures are apparent, not real. Every slip, every fall, every return to selfishness is a lesson learned, an experience gained, from which a golden grain of wisdom is extracted, helping the striver toward the accomplishment of his lofty object. To recognize this is to enter the way that leads unmistakably toward the divine.

Once come to regard your failings, your sorrows and sufferings, as so many voices telling you plainly where you are weak and faulty, where you fall below the true and the divine, you will then begin to ceaselessly watch yourself, and every slip, every pang of pain, will show you where you are to set to work and what you have to remove out of your heart in order to bring it nearer to the likeness of the Divine, nearer to the perfect love.

As you proceed, day by day detaching yourself more and more from the inward selfishness, the love that is selfless will gradually become revealed to you. And when you are growing patient and calm, when your petulance, tempers, and irritabilities are passing away from you, and the more powerful lusts and prejudices cease to dominate and enslave you, then you will know that the divine is awakening within you, that you are drawing near to the eternal heart, that you are not far from that selfless love, the possession of which is peace and immortality.

Divine love is distinguished from human loves in this supremely important particular: it is free from partiality. Human loves cling to a particular object to the exclusion of all else, and when that object is removed, great and deep is the resultant suffering to the one who loves. Divine love embraces the whole universe, and without clinging to any part yet contains within itself the whole. Those who come to it by gradually purifying and broadening their human loves until all the selfish and impure elements are burned out of them, cease from suffering. It is because human loves are narrow and confined and mingled with selfishness that they cause suffering. No suffering can result from that love which is so absolutely pure that it seeks nothing for itself. Nevertheless, human loves are absolutely necessary as steps toward the divine, and no soul is prepared to partake of divine love until it has become capable of the deepest and most intense human love. It is only by passing through human loves and human sufferings that divine love is reached and realized.

All human loves are perishable, like the forms to which they cling, but there is a love that is imperishable and that does not cling to appearances. All human loves are counterbalanced by human hates, but there is a love that admits of no opposite or reaction, divine and free from all taint of self, that sheds its fragrance on all alike. Human loves are reflections of the divine love and draw the soul nearer to the reality, the love that knows neither sorrow nor change.

It is well that the mother, clinging with passionate tenderness to the little helpless form of flesh that lies on her bosom, should be overwhelmed with the dark waters of sorrow when she sees it laid in the cold earth. It is well that her tears should flow and her heart ache, for only thus can she be reminded of the evanescent nature of the joys and objects of sense and be drawn nearer to the eternal and imperishable reality.

It is well that lover, brother, sister, husband, wife, should suffer deep anguish and be enveloped in gloom when the visible object of their affections is torn from them, so that they may learn to turn their affections toward the invisible Source of all, where alone abiding satisfaction is to be found.

It is well that the proud, the ambitious, the self-seeking, should suffer defeat, humiliation, and misfortune, that they should pass through the scorching fires of affliction, for only thus can the wayward soul be brought to reflect upon the enigma of life; only thus can the heart be softened and purified and prepared to receive the truth.

When the sting of anguish penetrates the heart of human love, when gloom and loneliness and desertion cloud the soul of friendship and trust, then it is that the heart turns toward the sheltering love of the Eternal and finds rest in its silent peace. And whosoever comes to this love is not turned away comfortless, is not pierced with anguish or surrounded with gloom, and is never deserted in the dark hour of trial.

The glory of divine love can only be revealed in the heart that is chastened by sorrow, and the image of the heavenly state can only be perceived and realized when the lifeless, formless accretions of ignorance and self are hewn away. Only that love that seeks no personal gratification or reward, that does not make distinctions, and that leaves behind no heartaches, can be called divine.

People, clinging to self and to the comfortless shadows of evil, are in the habit of thinking of divine love as something belonging to a God who is out of reach, as something outside themselves and that must forever remain outside. Truly, the love of God is ever beyond the reach of self, but when the heart and mind are emptied of self, then the selfless love, the supreme love, the love that is of God or good becomes an inward and abiding reality.

But how may one attain to this sublime realization? The answer which truth has always given and will ever give to this question is: "Empty thyself, and I will fill thee." Divine love cannot be known until self is dead, for self is the denial of love, and how can that which is known be also denied?

Those who have realized the love that is divine are reborn and cease to be swayed and dominated by the old elements of self. They are known for their patience, purity, self-control, deep charity of heart, and unalterable sweetness.

Divine or selfless love is not a mere sentiment or emotion; it is a state of knowledge which destroys the dominion of evil and the belief in evil and lifts the soul into the joyful realization of the supreme God. To the divinely wise, knowledge and love are one and inseparable.

It is toward the complete realization of this divine love that the whole world is moving; it was for this purpose that the universe came into existence, and every grasping at happiness, every reaching out of the soul toward objects, ideas, and ideals is an effort to realize it. But the world does not realize this love at present because it is grasping at the fleeting shadow and ignoring, in its blindness, the substance. And so suffering and sorrow continue and must continue until the world, taught by its self-inflicted pains, discovers the love that is selfless, the wisdom that is calm and full of peace.

And this love, this wisdom, this peace, this tranquil state of mind and heart, may be attained to, may be realized, by all who are willing and ready to yield up self and who are prepared to humbly enter into a comprehension of all that the giving up of self involves. There is no arbitrary power in the universe, and the strongest chains of fate by which people are bound are self-forged. They are chained to that which causes suffering because they desire to be so, because they love their chains, because they think their little dark prison of self is sweet and beautiful, and they are afraid that if they desert that prison, they will lose all that is real and worth having.

And the indwelling power which forged the chains and built around itself the dark and narrow prison can break away when it desires and wills to do so, and the soul does will to do so when it has discovered the worthlessness of its prison, when long suffering has prepared it for the reception of the boundless light and love.

As the shadow follows the form, and as smoke comes after fire, so effect follows cause, and suffering and bliss follow our thoughts and deeds. There is no effect in the world around us but has its hidden or revealed cause, and that cause is in accordance with absolute justice. People reap a harvest of suffering because in the near or distant past they have sown the seeds of evil; they reap a harvest of bliss also as a result of their own sowing of the seeds of good. Let us meditate upon this, let us strive to understand it, and we will then begin to sow only seeds of good and will burn up the tares and weeds which had formerly grown in the garden of our hearts.

The world does not understand the love that is selfless because it is engrossed in the pursuit of its own pleasures and cramped within the narrow limits of perishable interests, mistaking in its ignorance those pleasures and interests for real and abiding things. Caught in the flames of fleshly lusts and burning with anguish, it sees not the pure and peaceful beauty of truth. Feeding upon the swinish husks of error and self-delusion, it is shut out from the mansion of all-seeing love.

Not having this love, not understanding it, we institute innumerable reforms which involve no inward sacrifice, and we imagine that our reform is going to right the world forever, while we continue to propagate evil by engaging in it in our own hearts. That only can be called reform which tends to reform the human heart, for all evil has its rise there, and not until the world, ceasing from selfishness and party strife, has learned the lesson of divine love will it realize the golden age of universal blessedness.

Let the rich cease to despise the poor, and the poor

to condemn the rich; let the greedy learn how to give, and the lustful how to grow pure; let the partisan cease from strife, and the uncharitable begin to forgive; let the envious endeavor to rejoice with others, and the slanderers grow ashamed of their conduct. Let men and women take this course, and, lo! the Golden Age is at hand. Those who purify their own hearts are the world's greatest benefactors.

Yet though the world is and will be for many ages to come shut out from that "age of gold," which is the realization of selfless love, you, if you are willing, may enter it now by rising above your selfish self, if you will pass from prejudice, hatred, and condemnation, to gentle and forgiving love.

Where hatred, dislike, and condemnation are, selfless love does not abide. It resides only in the heart that has ceased from all condemnation. You say, "How can I love the drunkard, the hypocrite, the sneak, the murderer? I am compelled to dislike and condemn such people." It is true you cannot love such people emotionally, but when you say that you must perforce dislike and condemn them, you show that you are not acquainted with the great overruling love—for it is possible to attain to such a state of interior enlightenment as will enable you to perceive the train of causes by which these people have become as they are, to enter into their intense sufferings, and to know the certainty of their ultimate purification. Possessed of such knowledge it will be utterly impossible for you any longer to dislike or condemn them, and you will always think of them with perfect calmness and deep compassion.

If you love people and speak of them with praise until they in some way thwart you, or do something of which you disapprove, and then you dislike them and speak of them with dispraise, you are not governed by the love that is of God. If, in your heart, you are continually arraigning and condemning others, selfless love is hidden from you.

Those who know that love is at the heart of all things, and have realized the all-sufficing power of that love, have no room in their hearts for condemnation.

Those not knowing this love constitute themselves judge and executioner of others, forgetting that there is the Eternal Judge and Executioner, and insofar as people deviate from them in their own views, their particular reforms and methods, they brand them as fanatical, unbalanced, lacking judgment, sincerity, and honesty; insofar as others approximate to their own standard do they look upon them as being everything that is admirable. Such are those who are centered in self. But those whose hearts are centered in the supreme love do not so brand and classify others; do not seek to convert others to their own views, or to convince them of the superiority of their methods. Knowing the law of love, they live it and maintain the same calm attitude of mind and sweetness of heart toward all. The debased and the virtuous, the foolish and the wise, the learned and the unlearned, the selfish and the unselfish, receive alike the benediction of their tranquil thoughts.

You can only attain to this supreme knowledge, this divine love, by unremitting endeavor in self-discipline and by gaining victory after victory over yourself. Only the pure in heart see God, and when your heart is sufficiently purified, you will enter into the new birth and the love that does not die, or change, or end in pain and sorrow will be awakened within you and you will be at peace.

Those who strive for the attainment of divine love are ever seeking to overcome the spirit of condemnation, for where there is pure spiritual knowledge, condemnation cannot exist, and only in the heart that has become incapable of condemnation is love perfected and fully realized.

The Christian condemns the atheist; the atheist satirizes the Christian; the Catholic and Protestant are ceaselessly engaged in wordy warfare, and the spirit of strife and hatred rules where peace and love should be. Until you can regard people of all religions and of no religion with the same impartial spirit, with all freedom from dislike, and with perfect equanimity, you have yet to strive for that love which bestows upon its possessor freedom and salvation.

The realization of divine knowledge, selfless love, utterly destroys the spirit of condemnation, disperses all evil, and lifts the consciousness to that height of pure vision where love, goodness, and justice are seen to be universal, supreme, all-conquering, indestructible.

Train your mind in strong, impartial, and gentle thought; train your heart in purity and compassion; train your tongue to silence and to true and stainless speech; so shall you enter the way of holiness and peace and shall ultimately realize the immortal love. So living, without seeking to convert, you will convince; without arguing, you will teach; not cherishing ambition, the wise will find you out; and without striving to gain others' opinions, you will subdue their hearts. For love is all-conquering, all-powerful; and the thoughts, and deeds, and words of love can never perish.

To know that love is universal, supreme, all-sufficing; to be freed from the trammels of evil; to be quit of the inward unrest; to know that all people are striving to realize the truth each in his own way; to be satisfied, sorrowless, serene: this is peace; this is gladness; this is immortality; this is divinity; this is the realization of selfless love.

ENTERING INTO THE INFINITE

From the beginning of time, we, in spite of our bodily appetites and desires, in the midst of all our clinging to earthly and impermanent things, have ever been intuitively conscious of the limited, transient, and illusionary nature of our material existence, and in our sane and silent moments have tried to reach out into a comprehension of the Infinite, and have turned with tearful aspiration toward the restful reality of the eternal heart.

While vainly imagining that the pleasures of Earth are real and satisfying, pain and sorrow continually remind us of their unreal and unsatisfying nature. Ever striving to believe that complete satisfaction is to be found in material things, we are conscious of an inward and persistent revolt against this belief, which revolt is at once a refutation of our essential mortality and an inherent and imperishable proof that only in the immortal, the eternal, the Infinite can we find abiding satisfaction and unbroken peace.

And here is the common ground of faith; here the root and spring of all religion; here the soul of harmony and the heart of love—that we are essentially and spiritually divine and eternal and that, immersed in mortality and troubled with unrest, we are ever striving to enter into a consciousness of our real nature.

The human spirit is inseparable from the Infinite and can be satisfied with nothing short of the Infinite, and the burden of pain will continue to weigh upon our hearts and the shadows of sorrow to darken our pathway until, ceasing from our wanderings in the dream-world of matter, we come back to our home in the reality of the Eternal.

As the smallest drop of water detached from the ocean contains all the qualities of the ocean, so we, detached in consciousness from the Infinite, contain within ourselves its likeness; and as the drop of water must, by the law of its nature, ultimately find its way back to the ocean and lose itself in its silent depths, so must we, by the unfailing law of our nature, at last return to our source and lose ourselves in the great ocean of the Infinite.

To again become one with the Infinite is the goal of humankind. To enter into perfect harmony with the eternal law is wisdom, love, and peace. But this divine state is and must ever be incomprehensible to the merely personal. Personality, separateness, selfishness, are one and the same and are the antithesis of wisdom and divinity. By the unqualified surrender of the personality, separateness and selfishness cease, and we enter into the possession of our divine heritage of immortality and infinity.

Such surrender of the personality is regarded by the worldly and selfish mind as the most grievous of all calamities, the most irreparable loss, yet it is the one supreme and incomparable blessing, the only real and lasting gain. The mind unenlightened upon the inner laws of being, and upon the nature and destiny of its own life, clings to transient appearances, things that have in them no enduring substantiality, and so clinging, perishes, for the time being, amid the shattered wreckage of its own illusions.

We cling to and gratify the flesh as though it were going to last forever, and though we try to forget the nearness and inevitability of its dissolution, the dread of death and of the loss of all that we cling to clouds our happiest hours, and the chilling shadow of our own self-ishness follows us like a remorseless specter.

With the accumulation of temporal comforts and luxuries, the divinity within us is drugged, and we sink deeper and deeper into materiality, into the perishable life of the senses. Where there is sufficient intellect, the-ories concerning the immortality of the flesh come to be regarded as infallible truths. When our souls are clouded with selfishness in any or every form, we lose the power of spiritual discrimination and confuse the temporal with the eternal, the perishable with the per-manent, mortality with immortality, and error with truth. It is thus that the world has come to be filled with theories and speculations having no foundation in human experience. Every body of flesh contains within itself, from the hour of birth, the elements of its own destruction, and by the unalterable law of its own nature must it pass away.

The perishable in the universe can never become permanent; the permanent can never pass away; the mortal can never become immortal, the immortal can never die; the temporal cannot become eternal nor the eternal become temporal; appearance can never become reality, nor reality fade into appearance; error can never become truth, nor can truth become error. We cannot immortalize the flesh, but, by overcoming the flesh, by relinquishing all its inclinations, we can enter the region of immortality. "God alone hath immortality," and only by realizing the God state of consciousness do we enter into immortality.

All nature in its myriad forms of life is changeable, impermanent, unenduring. Only the informing principle of nature endures. Nature is many and is marked by separation. The informing principle is *one* and is marked by unity. By overcoming the senses and the self-ishness within, which is the overcoming of nature, we emerge from the chrysalis of the personal and illusionary and fly into the glorious light of the impersonal, the region of universal truth, out of which all perishable forms come.

Let us, therefore, practice self-denial; let us conquer our animal inclinations; let us refuse to be enslaved by luxury and pleasure; let us practice virtue and grow daily into higher and ever higher virtue, until at last we grow into the Divine and enter into both the practice and the comprehension of humility, meekness, forgiveness, compassion, and love, the practice and comprehension of which constitute Divinity.

"Goodwill gives insight," and only those who have

so conquered their personality that they have but one attitude of mind, that of goodwill toward all creatures, are possessed of divine insight and are capable of distinguishing the true from the false. Supremely good people are therefore wise, divine, enlightened, and have knowledge of the Eternal. Where you find unbroken gentleness, enduring patience, sublime lowliness, graciousness of speech, self-control, self-forgetfulness, and deep and abounding sympathy, look there for the highest wisdom; seek the company of such people, for they have realized the Divine; they live with the Eternal; they have become one with the Infinite. Eschew those who are impatient, given to anger, boastful, who cling to pleasure and refuse to renounce their selfish gratifications, and who practice not goodwill and far-reaching compassion, for such people do not have wisdom; all their knowledge is vain, and their works and words will perish, for they are grounded on that which passes away.

The world, the body, the personality, are mirages upon the desert of time, transitory dreams in the dark night of spiritual slumber, and those who have crossed the desert, those who are spiritually awakened, have alone comprehended the universal reality where all appearances are dispersed and dreaming and delusion are destroyed.

There is one great law that exacts unconditional obe-

dience, one unifying principle that is the basis of all
diversity, one eternal truth wherein all the problems of
Earth pass away like shadows. To realize this law, this
unity, this truth, is to enter into the Infinite, is to
become one with the Eternal.

To center one's life in the great law of love is to enter
into rest, harmony, and peace. To refrain from all partic-
ipation in evil and discord, to cease from all resistance to
evil, and from the omission of that which is good, and
to fall back upon unswerving obedience to the holy
calm within, is to enter into the inmost heart of things,
is to attain to a living, conscious experience of that eternal and infinite principle which must ever remain a hidden mystery to the merely perceptive intellect. Until this
principle is realized, the soul is not established in peace,
and those who so realize it are truly wise, not wise with
the wisdom of the learned but with the simplicity of a
blameless heart.

To enter into a realization of the Infinite and Eternal
is to rise superior to time, and the world, and the body,
which constitutes the kingdom of darkness; and is to
become established in immortality, Heaven, and the
Spirit, which make up the Empire of Light.

Entering into the Infinite is not a mere theory or
sentiment. It is a vital experience that is the result of

assiduous practice in inward purification. When the body is no longer believed to be, even remotely, your real self; when all appetites and desires are thoroughly subdued and purified; when the emotions are rested and calm; and when the oscillation of the intellect ceases and perfect poise is secured, then, and not till then, does consciousness become one with the Infinite; not until then is childlike wisdom and profound peace secured.

We grow weary and gray over the dark problems of life and finally pass away and leave them unsolved because we cannot see our way out of the darkness of the personality, being too much engrossed in its limitations. Seeking to save our personal lives, we forfeit the greater impersonal life in truth. Clinging to the perishable, we are shut out from knowledge of the Eternal.

By the surrender of self, all difficulties are overcome, and there is no error in the universe but the fire of inward sacrifice will burn it up like chaff; no problem, however great, but will disappear like a shadow under the searching light of self-abnegation. Problems exist only in our own self-created illusions, and they vanish away when self is yielded up. Self and error are synonymous. Error is involved in the darkness of unfathomable complexity, but eternal simplicity is the glory of truth.

Love of self shuts us out from truth, and seeking our

own personal happiness, we lose the deeper, purer, and more abiding bliss. Those who have yielded up that self, that personality that humankind most loves and to which they cling with such fierce tenacity, have left behind them all perplexity and have entered into a sim plicity so profoundly simple as to be looked upon by the world, involved as it is in a network of error, as foolishness. Yet such people have realized the highest wisdom and are at rest in the Infinite. They "accomplish without striving," and all problems melt before them, for they have entered the region of reality. They deal not with changing effects but with the unchanging principles of things. Having yielded up their lusts, errors, opinions, and prejudices, they have entered into possession of the knowledge of God, having slain the selfish desire for heaven along with it the ignorant fear of hell. Having relinquished even the love of life itself, they have gained supreme bliss and life eternal, the life which bridges life and death and knows its own immortality. Having yielded up all without reservation, they have gained all and rest in peace on the bosom of the Infinite.

Only those who have become so free from self as to be equally content to be annihilated as to live, or to live as to be annihilated, are fit to enter into the Infinite. Only those who, ceasing to trust their perishable self, have learned to trust in boundless measure the great law, the supreme Good, are prepared to partake of undying bliss.

For such people there is no more regret, or disappointment, or remorse, for where all selfishness has ceased, these sufferings cannot be; and whatever happens to them, they know that it is for their own good and they are content, being no longer the servant of self but the servant of the Supreme. They are no longer affected by the changes of Earth, and when they hear of wars, and rumors of wars their peace is not disturbed, and where others grow angry and cynical and quarrelsome, they bestow compassion and love. Though appearances may contradict it, they know that the world is progressing, and that

> Through its laughing and its weeping,
>   Through its living and its keeping,
>   Through its follies and its labors, weaving
>   in and out of sight,
>   To the end from the beginning,
>   Through all virtue and all sinning,
> Reeled from God's great spool of Progress,
>   runs the golden thread of light.

When a fierce storm is raging, none are angered about it because they know it will quickly pass away, and when the storms of contention are devastating the world, the sage, looking with the eye of truth and pity, knows that it will pass away and that, out of the wreckage of broken hearts which it leaves behind, the immortal Temple of Wisdom will be built.

Sublimely patient, infinitely compassionate, deep, silent, and pure, their very presence is a benediction. When they speak, their listeners ponder their words in their hearts and by them rise to higher levels of attainment. Such are they who have entered into the Infinite, who by the power of utmost sacrifice have solved the sacred mystery of life.

SAINTS, SAGES, AND SAVIORS: THE LAW OF SERVICE

The spirit of love that is manifested as a perfect and rounded life is the crown of being and the supreme end of knowledge upon this earth.

Truth is far removed from those whose life is not governed by love. The intolerant and condemnatory, even though they profess the highest religion, have the smallest measure of truth; while those who exercise patience and who listen calmly and dispassionately to all sides, and both arrive themselves at and incline others to, thoughtful and unbiased conclusions upon all problems and issues, have truth in fullest measure.

The final test of wisdom is this—How does a person live? What spirit is manifested? How are trials and temptations dealt with? Many people boast of being in possession of truth who are continually swayed by grief, disappointment, and passion, and who sink under the first little trial that comes along. Truth is nothing if not unchangeable, and insofar as a person takes a stand upon truth does that person become steadfast in virtue and rise superior to self-centered passions and emotions and changeable personality.

Perishable dogmas are formulated and called truth. Truth cannot be formulated; it is ineffable and ever beyond the reach of intellect. It can be experienced only by practice; it can be manifested only as a stainless heart and a perfect life.

Who then, in the midst of the ceaseless pandemonium of schools and creeds and parties, has the truth? Those who live it. Those who practice it. Those who, having risen above that pandemonium by overcoming their self-centeredness, no longer engage in it but sit apart, quiet, subdued, calm, and self-possessed, freed from all strife, all bias, all condemnation, and bestow upon all, the glad and unselfish love of the divinity within them.

Those who are patient, calm, gentle, and forgiving under all circumstances manifest the truth. Truth will never be proved by wordy arguments and learned treatises, for if people do not perceive the truth in infinite patience, undying forgiveness, and all-embracing compassion, no words can ever prove it to them.

It is an easy matter for the passionate to be calm and patient when they are alone or are in the midst of calmness. It is equally easy for the uncharitable to be gentle and kind when they are dealt kindly with, but those who retain their patience and calmness under all trial, who remain sublimely meek and gentle under the most trying circumstances, they and they alone are possessed of the spotless truth. And this is so because such lofty virtues belong to the Divine and can be manifested only by those who have attained to the highest wisdom, who have relinquished their passionate and self-seeking nature, who have realized the supreme and unchangeable law and have brought themselves into harmony with it.

Let us, therefore, cease from vain and passionate arguments about truth, and let them think and say and do those things which make for harmony, peace, love, and goodwill. Let them practice heart-virtue and search humbly and diligently for the truth that frees the soul from all error and sin, from all that blights the human heart, and that darkens, as with unending night, the pathway of the wandering souls of Earth.

There is one great all-embracing law, which is the

foundation and cause of the universe, *the law of love*. It has been called by many names in various countries and at various times, but behind all its names the same unalterable law may be discovered by the eye of truth. Names, religions, personalities, pass away, but the law of love remains. To become possessed of knowledge of this law, to enter into conscious harmony with it, is to become immortal, invincible, and indestructible.

It is because of the effort of the soul to realize this law that we humans come again and again to live, to suffer, and to die; and when realized, suffering ceases, personality is dispersed, and the fleshly life and death are destroyed, for consciousness becomes one with the Eternal.

This law is absolutely impersonal, and its highest manifested expression is that of service. When the purified heart has realized truth, it is then called upon to make the last, the greatest and holiest sacrifice, the sacrifice of the well-earned enjoyment of truth. It is by virtue of this sacrifice that the divinely emancipated soul comes to dwell among humankind, clothed with a body of flesh, content to dwell among the lowliest and least, and to be esteemed the servant of all humankind. That sublime humility which is manifested by the world's saviors is the seal of godhead, and those who have annihilated the personality and have become living, visible manifestations of the impersonal, eternal, boundless spirit of love are chosen as worthy to receive the unstinted worship of posterity. Only those who succeed in humbling themselves with that divine humility, which is not only the extinction of self but also the pouring out upon all the spirit of unselfish love, are exalted above measure and given spiritual dominion in the hearts of humankind.

All the great spiritual teachers have denied themselves personal luxuries, comforts, and rewards; have abjured temporal power and have lived and taught the limitless and impersonal truth. Compare their lives and teachings, and you will find the same simplicity, the same self-sacrifice, the same humility, love, and peace both lived and preached by them. They taught the same eternal principles, the realization of which destroys all evil. Those who have been hailed and worshipped as the saviors of humankind are manifestations of the great impersonal law and, being such, were free from passion and prejudice, and having no opinions and no special letter of doctrine to preach and defend, they never sought to convert and to proselytize. Living in the highest goodness, the supreme perfection, their sole object was to uplift humankind by manifesting that goodness in thought, word, and deed. They stand between the personal individual and the impersonal God and serve as exemplary types for the salvation of self-enslaved humankind.

People who are immersed in themselves, and who cannot comprehend the goodness that is absolutely impersonal, deny divinity to all saviors except their own, and thus introduce personal hatred and doctrinal controversy and, while defending their own particular views with passion, look upon each other as being heathens or infidels, and so render null and void, as far as their lives are concerned, the unselfish beauty and holy grandeur of the lives and teachings of their own masters. Truth cannot be limited; it can never be the special prerogative of any person, school, or nation, and when personality steps in, truth is lost.

The glory alike of saints, sages, and saviors is this—that they have realized the most profound lowliness, the most sublime unselfishness; having given up all, even their own personalities, all their works are holy and enduring, for they are freed from every taint of self. They give yet never think of receiving; they work without regretting the past or anticipating the future, and never look for reward.

When farmers have tilled and dressed the land and

put in the seed, they know that they have done all that they can possibly do and that they now must trust to the elements and wait patiently for the course of time to bring about the harvest, and that no amount of expectancy on their parts will affect the result. Even so, they who have realized truth go forth as sowers of the seeds of goodness, purity, love, and peace, without expectancy and never looking for results, knowing that there is the great overruling law which brings about its own harvest in due time and which is alike the source of preservation and destruction.

Most people do not understand the divine simplicity of a profound unselfish heart. They look upon their particular savior as the manifestation of a special miracle, as being something entirely apart and distinct from the nature of things and as being, in his ethical excellence, eternally unapproachable by the whole of humankind. This attitude of unbelief paralyzes effort and binds the souls of people as with strong ropes to sin and suffering. Jesus "grew in wisdom" and was "perfected by suffering." What Jesus was, he became such; what Buddha was, he became such; and every holy person became such by unremitting perseverance in self-sacrifice. Once recognize this, once realize that by watchful effort and hopeful perseverance you can rise above your lower nature, and great and glorious will be the vistas of attainment that will open out before you. Buddha vowed that he would not relax his efforts until he arrived at the state of perfection, and he accomplished his purpose.

What the saints, sages, and saviors have accomplished, you likewise may accomplish if you will only tread the way that they trod and pointed out, the way of self-sacrifice, of self-denying service.

Truth is very simple. It says, "Give up self," "Come unto Me" (away from all that defiles), "and I will give you rest." All the mountains of commentary that have been piled upon it cannot hide it from the heart that is earnestly seeking for righteousness. It does not require learning; it can be known in spite of learning. Disguised under many forms by erring, self-seeking people, the beautiful simplicity and clear transparency of truth remains unaltered and undimmed, and the unselfish heart enters into and partakes of its shining radiance. Not by weaving complex theories, not by building up speculative philosophies is truth realized; but by weaving the web of inward purity, by building up the temple of a stainless life is truth realized.

Those who enter upon this holy way begin by restraining their passions. This is virtue and is the beginning of saintliness, and saintliness is the beginning of holiness. Entirely worldly people gratify all their desires and practice no more restraint than the law of the land in which they reside demands. Virtuous people restrain their passions. Saints attack the enemy of truth in its stronghold within their own hearts and restrain all selfish and impure thoughts; while the holy ones are those who are free from passion and all impure thought and to whom goodness and purity have become as natural as scent and color are to the flower. The truly holy are divinely wise; they alone know truth in its fullness and have entered into abiding rest and peace. For them evil has ceased; it has disappeared in the universal light of the All-Good. Holiness is the badge of wisdom. Said Krishna to the Prince Arjuna:

> Humbleness, truthfulness, and harmlessness,
>   Patience and honor, reverence for the wise,
>   Purity, constancy, control of self,
>   Contempt of sense-delights, self-sacrifice,
>   Perception of the certitude of ill
>   In birth, death, age, disease, suffering, and
>   sin . . .
>   An ever-tranquil heart in fortunes good
>   And fortunes evil . . .
>   . . . endeavors resolute

> To reach perception of the Utmost Soul,
> And grace to understand what gain it were
> So to attain,—this is true Wisdom, Prince!
> And what is otherwise is ignorance!

Only the work that is impersonal can live; the works of self are both powerless and perishable. Where duties, howsoever humble, are done without self-interest and with joyful sacrifice, there is true service and enduring work. Where deeds, however brilliant and apparently successful, are done from love of self, there is ignorance of the law of service and the work perishes.

It is given to the world to learn one great and divine lesson, the lesson of absolute unselfishness. The saints, sages, and saviors of all time are they who have submitted themselves to this task and have learned and lived it. All the Scriptures of the world are framed to teach this one lesson; all the great teachers reiterate it. It is too simple for the world which, scorning it, stumbles along in the complex ways of selfishness.

A pure heart is the end of all religion and the beginning of divinity. To search for this righteousness is to walk the Way of Truth and Peace, and those who enter this Way will soon perceive that immortality which is independent of birth and death and will realize that in the divine economy of the universe the humblest effort is not lost.

The divinity of a Krishna, a Gautama, or a Jesus is the crowning glory of self-abnegation, the end of the soul's pilgrimage in matter and mortality, and the world will not have finished its long journey until every soul has become as these and has entered into the blissful realization of its own divinity.

THE REALIZATION OF
PERFECT PEACE

In the external universe there is ceaseless turmoil, change, and unrest; at the heart of all things there is undisturbed repose; in this deep silence dwells the Eternal.

We humans partake of this duality, and both the surface change and disquietude and the deep-seated eternal abode of Peace is contained within us.

As there are silent depths in the ocean which the fiercest storm cannot reach, so there are silent, holy depths in the human heart which the storms of sin and sorrow can never disturb. To reach this silence and to live consciously in it is peace.

Discord is rife in the outward world, but unbroken harmony holds sway at the heart of the universe. The human soul, torn by discordant passion and grief, reaches blindly toward the harmony of the sinless state, and to reach this state and to live consciously in it is peace.

Hatred severs human lives, fosters persecution, and hurls nations into ruthless war, yet we humans, though we do not understand why, retain some measure of faith in the overshadowing of a perfect love; and to reach this love and to live consciously in it is peace.

And this inward peace, this silence, this harmony, this love, is the Kingdom of Heaven, which is so difficult to reach because few are willing to give up themselves and to become as little children.

Heaven's gate is very narrow and minute.
    It cannot be perceived by foolish men
    Blinded by vain illusions of the world;
    E'en the clear-sighted who discern the way,
    And seek to enter, find the portal barred,
    And hard to be unlocked. Its massive bolts
Are pride and passion, avarice and lust.

We cry peace! peace! where there is no peace but on the contrary, discord, disquietude, and strife. Apart from that wisdom which is inseparable from self-renunciation, there can be no real and abiding peace.

The peace that results from social comfort, passing gratification, or worldly victory is transitory in its nature and is burned up in the heat of fiery trial. Only the Peace of Heaven endures through all trials, and only the selfless heart can know the Peace of Heaven.

Holiness alone is undying peace. Self-control leads to it, and the ever-increasing Light of Wisdom guides the pilgrim on the way. It is partaken of in a measure as soon as the path of virtue is entered upon, but it is realized in its fullness only when self disappears in the consummation of a stainless life.

> This is peace,
>> To conquer love of self and lust of life,
>> To tear deep-rooted passion from the heart
> To still the inward strife.

If you would realize the light that never fades, the joy that never ends, and the tranquility that cannot be disturbed; if you would leave behind forever your sins, your sorrows, your anxieties and perplexities; if you would partake of this salvation, this supremely glorious life, then conquer yourself. Bring every thought, every impulse, and every desire into perfect obedience to the divine power resident within you. There is no other way to peace but this, and if you refuse to walk it, your praying and your strict adherence to ritual will he fruitless and unavailing, and neither gods nor angels can help you. Come away, for a while, from external things, from the pleasures of the senses, from the arguments of the intellect, from the noise and the excitements of the world, and withdraw yourself into the inmost chamber of your heart, and there, free from the sacrilegious intrusion of all selfish desires, you will find a deep silence, a holy calm, a blissful repose, and if you will rest awhile in that holy place and will meditate there, the faultless eye of truth will open within you and you will see things as they really are. This holy place within you is your real and eternal self; it is the divine within you; and only when you identify yourself with it can you be said to be "clothed and in your right mind." It is the abode of peace, the Temple of Wisdom, the dwelling-place of immortality. Apart from this inward resting place, this Mount of Vision, there can be no true peace, no knowledge of the Divine, and if you can remain there for one minute, one hour, or one day, it is possible for you to remain there always.

All your sins and sorrows, your fears and anxieties, are your own, and you can cling to them or you can give them up. Of your own accord you cling to your unrest; of your own accord you can come to abiding peace. No one else can give up sin for you; you must give it up yourself. The greatest teacher can do no more than walk the way of truth and point it out to you; you yourself must walk it for yourself. You can obtain freedom and peace alone by your own efforts, by yielding up that which binds the soul and which is destructive of peace.

The angels of divine peace and joy are always at hand, and if you do not see them and hear them and dwell with them, it is because you shut yourself out from them and prefer the company of the spirits of evil within you. You are what you will to be, what you wish to be, what you prefer to be. You can commence to purify yourself and by so doing can arrive at peace, or you can refuse to purify yourself and so remain with suffering.

Step aside then; come out of the fret and the fever of life, away from the scorching heat of self, and enter the inward resting place where the cooling airs of peace will calm, renew, and restore you.

Come out of the storms of sin and anguish. Why be

troubled and tempest-tossed when the haven of peace is so near?

Give up all self-seeking; give up self and the Peace of God will be yours!

Subdue the animal within you; conquer every selfish uprising, every discordant voice; transmute the base metals of your selfish nature into the unalloyed gold of love and you shall realize the life of perfect peace. Thus subduing, thus conquering, thus transmuting, you will, while living in the flesh, cross the dark waters of mortality and will reach that shore upon which the storms of sorrow never beat, and where sin and suffering and dark uncertainty cannot come. Standing upon that shore, holy, compassionate, awakened, self-possessed, and glad with unending gladness, you will realize that

> Never the Spirit was born, the Spirit will cease to
>> be never;
>> Never was time it was not, end and beginning
>>> are dreams;
>> Birthless and deathless and changeless remaineth
>>> the Spirit forever;
> Death hath not touched it at all, dead though the
>> house of it seems.

You will then know the meaning of sin, of sorrow, of suffering, and that the end thereof is wisdom. You will know the cause and the issue of existence.

And with this realization you will enter into rest, for this is the bliss of immortality, this is the unchangeable gladness, this is the untrammeled knowledge, undefiled wisdom, and undying love; this, and this only, is the realization of perfect peace.

ABOUT THE AUTHORS

James Allen was born in Leicester, England, in 1864. He took his first job at fifteen to support his family, after his father was murdered while looking for work in America. Allen worked as a private secretary with various manufacturing companies until 1902, when he left to devote himself fully to writing. Shortly after completing his first book, *From Poverty to Power,* in 1901, he moved to Ilfracombe, England, where he went on to write eighteen more books before his death in 1912. Originally published in 1903, *As a Man Thinketh* is his second and most widely celebrated work, cited by generations of prosperity authors.

ARTHUR R. PELL, PH.D., is the revising author of the widely popular updated edition of Napoleon Hill's *Think and Grow Rich*. He has also written numerous books on management and career planning, including *The Complete Idiot's Guide to Managing People* and *The Complete Idiot's Guide to Team Building*. Pell was the editor in charge of updating Dale Carnegie's classic *How to Win Friends and Influence People*. He lives in Hartsdale, New York.

Look for these Prosperity Favorites from Tarcher/Penguin

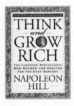

Think and Grow Rich by Napoleon Hill
The landmark guide by the champion wealth-builder of all time—now revised and updated for the twenty-first century.
ISBN 978-1-58542-433-7

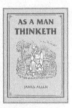

As a Man Thinketh by James Allen
The beloved classic on the creative potential of the human mind—available in a beautiful early replica edition.   ISBN 978-1-58542-564-8

Creative Mind and Success by Ernest Holmes
A slender volume of immense power on the mental principles of success, by the author of *The Science of Mind*.   ISBN 978-1-58542-608-9

Your Magic Power to be Rich! By Napoleon Hill
The ultimate all-in-one prosperity bible, featuring updated editions of Hill's great works *Think and Grow Rich, The Magic Ladder to Success, and The Master-Key to Riches.*
ISBN 978-1-58542-555-6

Relax into Wealth by Alan Cohen
One of today's top life coaches explores the hidden key to success: Being yourself.
ISBN 978-1-58542-563-1

The Circle by Laura Day
The treasured guidebook that shows how the power of one simple wish can transform your entire life.   ISBN 978-1-58542-598-3